Praise for

"As a journalist, I see the
choices. *Reaching Your Pr*
hope and healing to parents who have more questions than answers."

Gretchen Carlson

Host of *The Real Story with Gretchen Carlson* on Fox News
and Best-Selling Author of *Getting Real*

"*Reaching Your Prodigal* is an honest but tender book filled with wisdom."

Candace Cameron Bure

Actress, Author, Cohost of *The View*

"Loving a son or daughter is not always as simple as it may seem. Harsh words and wrong choices can separate relationships in a way that may seem unrepairable. In *Reaching Your Prodigal*, Phil Waldrep offers understanding, encouragement, and real solutions to parents who want to do the right thing but are not quite sure exactly what that might be. This book is a must!"

Andy Andrews

New York Times Best-Selling Author of
The Traveler's Gift and *The Noticer*

"Parenting a prodigal is heartbreaking on so many levels. Phil Waldrep offers an insightful, practical guide for grandparents and parents everywhere. Hopeful and encouraging, this book provides the answers you've been looking

Author of

D1316395

"*Reaching Your Prodigal* helps you extend grace while making tough decisions when dealing with your own prodigal. There is hope!"

Michael W. Smith
Singer/Songwriter

"The passion of Phil Waldrep to give parents and grandparents help in relating to their prodigals is evident on every page of *Reaching Your Prodigal*. Readers will find biblically based principles giving hope on every page."

Pat Williams
Orlando Magic Cofounder and Senior Vice President
and Author of *Extreme Winning*

"In *Reaching Your Prodigal*, Phil Waldrep provides wise direction and uncommon good sense for parents and grandparents struggling with a prodigal. Using rich, biblical examples and powerful, real-life stories, Phil helps you work through the guilt and heartache and press on to do what's best for your prodigal and for you. Compassion and grace are poured across every page. You will be comforted and encouraged, yet challenged as well. I believe this valuable resource is going to set people free. Highly recommended!"

Liz Curtis Higgs
Best-Selling Author of *Bad Girls of the Bible*

"Having a prodigal son or daughter may be one of the most helpless feelings on earth. In *Reaching Your Prodigal,* Phil Waldrep offers practical help and hope that will be a life changer for many families."

Ken Davis
Award-Winning Speaker, Author, and Trainer

"*Reaching Your Prodigal* is one of the best books I have ever read in regards to reaching our loved ones. I've been there . . . and I'm glad I read Phil's insights beforehand. What a joy it was when my loved ones returned home! So, while you're waiting on the porch . . . grab a cup of coffee and read *Reaching Your Prodigal* . . . and from time to time . . . look down the dusty road . . . they may be coming home!"

Dr. Dennis Swanberg
America's Minister of Encouragement

"I always tell parents of teenagers that we go through labor twice with our children, and that the second time—beginning with their puberty—lasts about eight years. If you're somewhere in the middle of that groaning, pushing, screaming, waiting, marveling experience, you'll want to read *Reaching Your Prodigal* by my friend Phil Waldrep. It's a wonderful, thoughtful, in-some-places-humorous, in-all-places-practical mix of counsel, advice, and encouragement. Part pastor, part experienced parent, and part midwife (!), Phil gives us just the coaching we need in the labor process of parenting adolescents. Read, push, practice your breathing, and watch for a miracle."

Dr. Duffy Robbins
Professor of Youth Ministry at Eastern University

"*Reaching Your Prodigal* is a treasure trove of godly wisdom and practical advice. Phil Waldrep has written a wonderful resource for those who love and pray for prodigals. Whether you are a pastor, counselor, parent, or maybe even a prodigal yourself, this book will be a comforting guide for you."

Jan Silvious
Author, Speaker, Coach

"Having been a family life educator for over four decades, it is always exciting to find a resource that I can recommend. Phil Waldrep merges sound scriptural interpretation, healthy psychological insights, and practical solutions to address two fundamental questions faced by most families. I have given away many copies of *Reaching Your Prodigal,* which underscores my confidence that it can profoundly help individuals and families traveling through the valley of shadows."

Charles V. Petty, PhD
President of Family Success Unlimited

"You'll find tremendous encouragement in the pages of *Reaching Your Prodigal,* in which Phil Waldrep offers real and relevant hope for families who are praying their prodigal home."

Babbie Mason
Singer/Songwriter and Author

"With his latest book, *Reaching Your Prodigal,* Phil Waldrep brings hope, encouragement, and godly advice to each of us who daily struggle with the pain of having a prodigal in our lives. Pick it up, read it, and let the Lord use this monograph to begin the process of healing and hope in your life and in the life of your prodigal."

Mark H. Ballard
President of Northeastern Baptist College

"In *Reaching Your Prodigal,* all you have to do is read the chapter titles to know Phil Waldrep has written a practical book to help each of us reach the prodigals in our lives."

Gigi Graham
Daughter of Billy Graham

"*Reaching Your Prodigal* is a powerful gift to the church. Thank you, Phil, for writing this brave, honest, and incredibly helpful book."

David Nasser

Author, Speaker, and

Liberty University Sr. VP for Spiritual Development

"This is one of the most practical and relevant books I have ever read. Phil Waldrep shows you, through refreshing biblical truths, how to turn a ruined relationship into a loving, intimate family bond."

Josh McDowell

Josh McDowell Ministries, Dallas, Texas

"Whether you're the prodigal or longing for the return of one, there's a heavenly Father who understands and shares your pain. Heartfelt thanks to Phil Waldrep for reminding us that God's Word is filled with hope and encouragement for those who have 'left' and for those who continue to wait!"

Cindi Wood

Author of the Frazzled Female Series and

Anonymous: Discovering the Somebody You Are to God

"This wise book is essential for every parent who watches and wonders when or if their prodigal will 'come home' in their beliefs and actions. Phil Waldrep illustrates in very practical ways how to reach a prodigal through compassion and communication, not condemnation. He also demonstrates, biblically, that parents should not blame themselves for their child's choices. Most important, this book offers great hope—for them and for you."

Shaunti Feldhahn

Social Researcher and Best-Selling Author of

For Women Only and *For Parents Only*

REACHING YOUR
PRODIGAL

What Did I Do Wrong? What Do I Do Now?

PHIL WALDREP

WORTHY®
PUBLISHING

Published by Worthy Books, an imprint of Worthy Publishing Group, a division of Worthy Media, Inc., One Franklin Park, 6100 Tower Circle, Suite 210, Franklin, TN 37067.

WORTHY is a registered trademark of Worthy Media, Inc.

HELPING PEOPLE EXPERIENCE THE HEART OF GOD

eBook available wherever digital books are sold.

Library of Congress Cataloging-in-Publication Data

Names: Waldrep, Phil, author.
Title: Reaching your prodigal : answers to parents' questions : "What did I do wrong?" and "What can I do now?" / Phil Waldrep.
Description: Franklin, TN : Worthy Publishing Group, a division of Worthy Media, Inc., [2015]
Identifiers: LCCN 2015043767 | ISBN 9781617956751 (tradepaper)
Subjects: LCSH: Parent and adult child--Religious aspects--Christianity. | Ex-church members. | Non-church-affiliated people.
Classification: LCC BV4529 .W255 2015 | DDC 248.8/45--dc23

Unless otherwise noted, Scripture taken from the New King James Version®. Copyright © 1982 by Thomas Nelson. Used by permission. All rights reserved.

Scripture quotations marked ESV are taken from The Holy Bible, English Standard Version® (ESV®), copyright © 2001 by Crossway, a publishing ministry of Good News Publishers. Used by permission. All rights reserved.

For foreign and subsidiary rights, contact rights@worthypublishing.com

The author expresses his gratitude to the people who shared their stories in this book. To protect their privacy, the author changed many of the names, places, and details not affecting the illustration.

ISBN: 978-1-61795-675-1

Cover Design: Tobias' Outerwear for Books
Cover Image: Photocase.com

Printed in the United States of America
16 17 18 19 20 VPI 8 7 6 5 4 3 2

For Debbie, Maegan, Melodi, T.C., and Emory

Contents

· · · · — — · · ·

FOREWORD

· · · · — — · · ·

ONE OF THE GREATEST PROBLEMS facing evangelicals in today's culture is the disconnect between generations. Truths held dear by one generation are being jettisoned by the next. Sometimes the younger generation points its finger at the lack of integrity in the lifestyle of their parents. But often there is no perceptible cause-and-effect relationship.

Like the young man from the New Testament who demanded his inheritance and took off for the far country, many of our young people today are simply denying their spiritual heritage and choosing to live apart from the Lord.

It is easy to diagnose the problem. It is not as easy to provide a solution. Fortunately, my friend Phil Waldrep has done an excellent job in this invaluable resource for families. His six principles provide insight, encouragement, and hope for every parent, grandparent, or sibling who loves a prodigal.

On several occasions, I have invited Phil to speak to the people of Shadow Mountain Community Church. His ministry and words of encouragement to us have led me to expect nothing but excellence from whatever he does.

Reaching Your Prodigal certainly measures up to his high standard. From the heart and perspective of a caring servant, Phil has taken a problem that is often neglected and given it the serious treatment it deserves.

Whether you find yourself parenting a prodigal, or you know someone who is, I guarantee that this book will bring help and hope. Read it prayerfully, and ask God to give you the courage to implement its life-changing principles.

Dr. David Jeremiah
Turning Point Ministries
San Diego, California
December 7, 2015

Chapter 1

. . . . — — . . .

UNDERSTANDING
YOUR PAIN

IT IS THE EYES that give me the first clue.

When I see their faces, I immediately know: this man or woman is grieving.

They are not grieving because someone died. Ask them, though, and they will tell you the pain is just as real.

They have a prodigal in their family. It might be a son or daughter who walked away from his or her faith in God, or a grandchild who is choosing to avoid the church. It could be a sibling who is isolating herself from the influence of her family. For others, it is a mom or dad—once faithful in their Christian commitment—who now has no interest in spiritual matters.

The pain these men and women feel is intense. In some cases, it is paralyzing them emotionally.

I received a letter a few years ago that turned my attention to exploring answers to the questions these family members were asking.

The words of this letter echo the pain that I often hear.

Dear Phil,

I am writing you this letter this morning because my heart is very heavy. I've been carrying a burden for a long time, and I don't know where to turn for help. I've wanted to talk to people in my church about it, but if I do, I'm afraid it will become the subject of gossip. I'm not sure I can stand that, so I'm sharing my heart with you, hoping you can give me some advice. You spoke in our church a few months ago, and we enjoyed listening to you very much. After church, you came to our house for lunch. You saw a photograph of my husband and me with our five grown sons, and you asked about them. For the next few minutes, I told you about them—well, about four of them, anyway. The three oldest live with their wives and children in Birmingham, where they were born and grew up before my husband was transferred. They are all fine young men, very much involved in their churches. Our youngest son married a pretty girl, a Methodist, and they now attend a Methodist church in Jackson. (I tease him that now he's a missionary to the Methodists.)

But Phil, I didn't tell you anything about our fourth son, Morris. Either you didn't notice, or you were gracious enough not to ask. Like the other boys, he grew up in church. Every time the doors were open, we were there. He heard the message of Christ loudly, clearly, and often. Morris was a loveable boy, and he sang in the choir. He volunteered to speak at every year's Youth Sunday. In fact, when the boys were young, I told my friends that he would be the one who would become a preacher or a missionary. He had such a sweet spirit.

After Morris graduated from high school, he went to college. For the first couple of years, he remained faithful to God, but then, something happened. I'm not sure what it was, but something turned his heart cold. When he came home on some weekends, we noticed that he didn't sing the hymns, and he backed away from my friends he had hugged only a few months before. I thought this was just one of those "phases" we hear about.

A few weeks later, a friend called us. His daughter went to the same university, and she had told her parents that Morris had been drinking and partying a lot. We were shocked, but when we tried to talk to him about it, he shook his head. He didn't want to talk about his drinking. Instead, he dropped a bomb on us. He told us that he was getting married—in two weeks. You guessed it. She was pregnant.

Morris quit college just before his senior year. His wife had the baby, and they seemed to be doing well, considering the circumstances. After about two years, though, he told his wife he didn't love her anymore, and he moved out. We found out later that he was having an affair with a woman he worked with.

He moved to get farther away from us and from his wife and child. We see him about every three months, and we talk to him on the phone almost every week, but he has made it clear that he doesn't want to talk to us about the Lord, church, or his decisions that have caused us and him so much pain. We recently learned that he is living with a woman, and they aren't married.

Phil, I'm struggling. How can a child grow up hearing the message of the gospel, have four brothers who love God and parents who would die for him, and end up so far away from God? Isn't there a verse in the Bible that says if we had raised him right he'd be serving the Lord today? I'm sure I've heard people quote that verse many times over the years, and it cuts my heart like a knife. What I really want to know is, what did I do wrong, and what can we do now to help our son return to God? Even if you don't have any advice, would you please pray for us?

Thank you for reading my letter and sharing our pain.

Sincerely yours,
Dorothy

Is it possible this could be your letter with some minor changes? For you, it might be daughters instead of sons or two children instead of five. Maybe the problem with your prodigal is drugs or a prison sentence instead of an unwanted pregnancy. The one trait you have in common with Dorothy is you love someone who decided to walk away from God. Now that person's choice is causing you pain.

You, no doubt, are asking the same questions this dear lady asked in her letter:

How can it happen to me?

What did I do wrong?

And what can I do now to bring the prodigal I love back into a right relationship with God?

After reading the letter, I determined I was going to find answers to these questions. I did what every researcher would do. I looked for books to find principles to share with hurting parents. I searched for sermons that explained biblical reasons for the prodigal's behavior. I scanned magazines, all in hopes of finding insights to share with family members seeking answers.

To my surprise, I found only a few books and a handful of magazine articles about the subject. Unfortunately, most of these discussed the sociological and psychological effects of deviant behavior without addressing the root causes. Some told the story of a prodigal, either from the child's viewpoint or the parents. But, it seemed, no one wanted to address the most important questions: Why? and What now?

I kept Dorothy's letter in my computer bag for weeks. Several times I tried to respond, but answers to her questions eluded me. Over time, her concern became a burden. In fact, it became an obsession. I had to know why someone reared in a godly family would decide to ignore their spiritual heritage and begin making poor decisions. Most importantly, I had to know what parents had to do to get their wayward child back.

I searched the Word of God looking for answers. I examined every verse written about rebellion. Every biblical personality noted as running from God was the subject of my personal study. Although I understood the verses and the stories, the answers remained unclear.

My initial response was to back away. Having entered the ministry at an early age, I couldn't relate on a firsthand basis with the thinking of a "classical" prodigal. Granted, I have not lived a perfect life, but the logic of going against the moral principles of Scripture for a long time did not resonate with me. I could not write from experience. For me, there was no way to find the answers I wanted by exploring the thoughts and feelings of a prodigal.

Until, that is, I finished speaking to a group of older adults one night in a small town in Missouri. My assignment was to have a lighthearted time of encouragement by getting the attendees to laugh at some of the problems of aging. For nearly forty-five minutes laughter filled the room.

When we concluded, an elderly lady stood near the door. As I was getting ready to leave, she approached me and asked if she could speak to me privately. We stepped away from the crowd. She shared that the Lord impressed her to ask me to pray for her daughter. She briefly told me the painful story of her daughter's destructive behavior.

Then she repeated almost verbatim the questions in Dorothy's letter. "Phil," she said as tears filled her eyes, "what did I do wrong with my daughter? And please tell me, what can I do to get her to stop destroying her life and start serving the Lord again?"

I could not answer her questions. All I could do was assure her of my continued prayers for her and her daughter.

As I drove back to the hotel where I was staying, those questions became louder in my mind. Although I was alone in the car, it felt like passengers were in every seat screaming, "What did I do wrong?" and "What can I do to change this situation?"

I remember walking into the hotel room, tossing my

jacket across the chair, and falling across the bed. For the next few minutes I cried out to God. "Please, Lord," I prayed, "give me insight to help these hurting people, or remove this burden from my heart. I cannot continue hearing their pain and not being able to help."

I went to bed a brief time later and, being tired from a long day, I fell asleep.

Around two in the morning my eyes opened, and suddenly I had an idea. I leaped from the bed, grabbed a pen and paper, and began writing. No, I was not writing ideas or thoughts. I started writing names. I listed the names of every person I knew well who was a prodigal or had been a prodigal in recent years.

When I completed writing all the names on the list, there were thirty people representing every type of prodigal you could imagine. Some were good, moral people who no longer had an interest in attending church. Others battled addictions and various problems. One was incarcerated for committing a serious felony.

When I returned home from my trip, I contacted every person on my list. I asked if they would be willing to meet with me. All agreed. Over the next few months I interviewed these thirty prodigals and listened to their stories. I offered no comments. I only asked questions.

As I reviewed their responses and recalled the scriptures

I studied, everything came into focus. There, before my eyes, were the principles for getting a prodigal back to God.

Our heavenly Father feels the pain you are experiencing. Your prodigal is breaking His heart too. When you weep, He feels the warmth of your tears. When you cry out that you cannot take it anymore, He hears your voice. Believe me— He wants the one you love back in a right relationship with Him more than you do.

To help us understand what is happening around us and why, Jesus told a story in the fifteenth chapter of the gospel of Luke about a son who went his own way.

Although the Bible does not use the word *prodigal* to describe the young man, most people refer to it as the story of the prodigal son. *Prodigal* originates from a Latin word meaning "wasteful." Today we use the term to refer to anyone who wastes his money, his time, or his life.

Jesus always had a reason for telling a story. The day He told about this rebellious son was no different. In fact, it was the third of three stories Jesus told in one setting.

The first story was about a shepherd who rejoiced when he found a lost sheep. The second one was about a woman who was happy when she found a lost coin. Against this backdrop of two people losing and finding something precious, Jesus told the third story. It was about a son who walked away from his father's love and acceptance.

All three stories were a word picture of how God values us. Our refusal to love and honor Him breaks His heart. His love and persistent concern for us demonstrates how much He longs for prodigals to return to Him.

It is common to focus on the son when you read this story. As you read it again, I want you to focus on the words and actions of the father, not the son. When you do, you will understand why I refer to it as The Story of a Wonderful Father rather than The Story of the Prodigal Son.

Luke recorded the words of Jesus as the story begins: "A certain man had two sons. And the younger of them said to his father, 'Father, give me the portion of goods that falls to me.' And he divided to them his livelihood" (Luke 15:11–12).

From all accounts, the father was a wealthy man. It was the Jewish custom of this era for the oldest heir to receive two-thirds of an estate upon the death of his father. The other heirs divided the remainder. Since there were only two sons, the youngest son would receive one-third.

Instead of waiting for his father to die, the youngest son requested his father give him his inheritance in advance. The son made the decision to leave and take his part of the estate with him.

The father had every right to deny his request. It might mean his son physically stayed home but his heart would not be there. The father allowed his adult son to make his own decisions. The father did not agree or approve of his actions, but he granted his request.

Whatever he got from his father, he sold.

The story continues. "And not many days after, the younger son gathered all together, journeyed to a far country, and there wasted his possessions with prodigal living" (v. 13).

In the mind of prodigals, the best place to be is away from any moral authority they dislike. "A far country" was a literal place to this young man. It separated him physically from his father. Regardless of where prodigals are physically, emotional and spiritual separation creates a false feeling of happiness.

The prodigal soon discovered all decisions, good or bad, have consequences.

"But when he had spent all, there arose a severe famine in that land, and he began to be in want. And he went and joined himself to a citizen of that country, and he sent him into his fields to feed swine. And he would gladly have filled his stomach with the pods that the swine ate, and no one gave him anything" (vv. 14–16).

Every prodigal reaches a point when his fun turns to a famine. Wrong decisions lead to emotional bankruptcy. God, in His wisdom, designed the consequences of sin to make us desperate. Prodigals often try to fill the void with whatever they can find. Sometimes it is stronger drugs, another relationship, or moving farther away. With time, they start living in a pigpen alone. No one around them cares if they live or die.

Back at home, the prodigal's father continued to grieve. It is possible word reached him that his son was feeding pigs. For a Jewish man, having a son associated with pigs was the worst shame a parent could experience. Culturally, it was worse than any addiction, criminal behavior, or sexual immorality.

The father probably considered all his options. Would it help if he sent money? What if a servant took the boy some food? True, it would get his son out of the pigpen. The family's shame might end, but he would remain a prodigal. The son would not be home.

No one knows how long the son was gone. As the years probably passed, the father evaluated every past activity. Did he do the right thing by giving him his inheritance? What if he'd talked more when the boy was a teenager or scrutinized his friends closer? Would things be different now?

Guilt probably plagued the father.

Time passed. Finally the prodigal reached a point where his desperation turned to brokenness.

"And when he came to himself, he said, 'How many of my father's hired servants have bread enough and to spare, and I perish with hunger! I will arise and go to my father, and will say to him, "Father, I have sinned against heaven and before you, and I am no longer worthy to be called your son. Make me like one of your hired servants"'" (vv. 17–19).

The wise father knew brokenness was the only remedy to the pride of his son. Only brokenness would make the son think of home. Fortunately, the father made sure no barriers existed to prevent his son from returning.

The greatest struggle for any parent of a prodigal is waiting for brokenness to come. Though you may try, you cannot rush the process. Nagging a prodigal to read a book or begging him to go to church will not speed brokenness. In fact, it can drive him further away.

Brokenness brings prodigals to the end of their rope. Prodigals tend to stay in the "far country" as long as they have some rope left. When parents provide more rope, they postpone the beginning of brokenness. Trying to remove the rope they have, however, will erect a barrier if loved ones are not careful.

Brokenness prompts a desire in our hearts to be restored. This prodigal's first thought of restoration was family, and in this case his father came to mind.

The hardest moment for prodigals is when they admit their error. Like their decisions of the past, they cannot predict or control what will happen.

What would his father say? How would the family react?

Prodigals think they may have only one opportunity to find grace in the family's eyes. For that reason, they contemplate the moment they admit their wrong.

In the story Jesus told, the son rehearsed the speech to his father. He would ask his father only for food and shelter. True repentance never demands. It only requests. "And he arose and came to his father. But when he was still a great way off, his father saw him and had compassion, and ran and fell on his neck and kissed him" (v. 20).

If the excitement of leaving is the emotional high for a prodigal, the embarrassment of returning is the emotional low. With his emotions raw, what would be the emotions of his father? Would he be angry? Would his father shame him before the servants?

As the prodigal looked into the eyes of his father, he began his speech.

"And the son said to him, 'Father, I have sinned against heaven and in your sight, and am no longer worthy to be called your son.' But the father said to his servants, 'Bring out the best robe and put it on him, and put a ring on his hand and sandals on his feet. And bring the fattened calf here and kill it, and let us eat and be merry; for this my son was dead and is alive again; he was lost and is found.' And they began to be merry" (vv. 21–24).

The reunion described by Jesus is the desire of every person who loves a prodigal. Unknown to most, it also is the longing of every broken prodigal. For prodigals, they come with the hope of grace. For family members, they come with the grace of hope. Love motivates both.

Before the reunion, the prodigal's actions were the most important. Once the reunion occurred, it was the father's reactions that took the lead. The father in this story restored the dignity of the repentant son.

The overjoyed parent ordered the servants to bring a robe, a ring, and some shoes. The best robe in the house was for an honored guest. The ring signified his position as a son, and his sandals meant that he was not a slave.

Best of all, a celebration occurred.

Sure, the father could demand answers or list the ways his son brought shame to the family. He refused the urge. The father used wisdom when the son left, and now he exercised it when he returned.

The oldest son failed to understand the attention his father was giving his brother. It did not seem fair.

The celebration started the healing process. The days ahead would be difficult.

Repentant prodigals often open old wounds buried by family members. Wisdom must navigate the waters after prodigals return as much as when they were away.

The story Jesus told illustrates how sinful behavior affects more than the parents. It affects siblings, grandparents, and friends. In some cases, it is the grandparent or friend who has the burden for the prodigal, not a parent.

Regardless of your relationship to a prodigal, the principles we will examine challenge you to be honest. You will see your limitations and your possibilities. Best of all, in the pages ahead you will find hope.

- -

TRUTH TO REMEMBER

God values you and your prodigal. He desires a change in your prodigal's heart as much as you do.

- -

Chapter 2

· · · — — · · ·

SEEING YOUR PRODIGAL

YOU HAVE A PRODIGAL. You know it and others know it.

When you are around an acquaintance and your prodigal is mentioned, how do you respond? It probably depends on the type of prodigal in your life.

We tend to think of prodigals as rebellious people. We see them as angry children who leave home or addicts who refuse to listen. In the minds of most, the word *prodigal* often appears in the same paragraph as the words *jail* or *treatment*.

Prodigals, however, come in various types.

For example, your prodigal might be

- an embarrassing prodigal,
- a defiant prodigal,
- an intellectual prodigal,
- a complacent prodigal, or
- a religious prodigal.

By no means is this list exhaustive. Most prodigals, however, can be put in one of these general categories.

EMBARRASSING PRODIGALS

Take, for example, the embarrassing prodigal.

This could be a son who is in prison or a daughter living with her boyfriend. It might be your grandchild who is in drug rehab. The inventory of sins they commit is endless. Their defining characteristic is behavior that is public and shameful.

Having an embarrassing prodigal in your family is hard. Their behavior makes them (and you) a prime target for gossip.

Parents often try to defend the character of a prodigal when someone asks about them. They remind everyone that "she is a good girl, just running with the wrong crowd." Sometimes we try to hide the truth.

Jerry has a son who is serving ten years in prison for burglary. The young man often works as a member of the prison's chain gang cleaning state highways. When people ask the father where his son works, he replies, "He is working for the state."

If their actions are too obvious to defend, you try to evade the question or change the subject. You know people are talking. Most of the time it is to others, not you. So you may go to great lengths to keep from facing people.

One family had a member who was a male prostitute. When he announced his homosexuality, some family members did not know how to react. Later, when he acknowledged his profession, shame filled their hearts. They could not comprehend how something like this could happen in their family. Many of his relatives refused to attend family reunions, just to avoid him.

A few years later, the man died of AIDS. Even then, his family tried to avoid facing citizens of the community. After his death, the family rushed to bury him. No one announced his funeral. Close family members gathered briefly at his graveside. Most never spoke of him again. The embarrassment was more than they could bear.

Occasionally friends intentionally bring the embarrassment to us. If the actions of the prodigal affected them, they quickly demand restitution. Embarrassing reminders is their weapon of choice.

Danny grew up attending church in a small Mississippi town, his family going regularly throughout his childhood. After he graduated from college, the church asked him to return and serve as their music director. His parents beamed with pride every Sunday when he led the choir.

After serving for three years, the young man embezzled some church funds. The church leadership was furious. Their anger, however, was not toward the worship leader. The leaders blamed his parents. "If he had been raised right," several of them said, "he wouldn't have done such an awful thing."

His parents continued to attend the church. Every Sunday they faced the gossip of their friends. Even though they never condoned their son's actions, the unkind words embarrassed them. One leader said to his father, "I know he's a grown man, but he's your son. If you're the man you ought to be, you'll write the church a check to cover what he stole." The father, wanting the embarrassment to end, took out a second mortgage on his home and wrote the check.

Families with embarrassing prodigals sometimes feel isolated. They cannot change the problem, so they suffer alone.

Ruth Ann is a precious lady whose son committed a murder. For years she endured trials and appeals. She regularly traveled to visit her son. Finally, the worst day of her life came when the state executed him for his crime. A doctor injected a needle into his arm, and moments later he was dead. That afternoon, Ruth Ann wept alone.

I recall Ruth Ann's words about her ordeal. She said, with tears streaming down her face, "In all those years, I don't remember anyone who came to me and told me, 'I know you are hurting. I am praying for you.'" Prideful citizens, though, made sure she heard, "Your son is getting exactly what he deserves."

For most parents with embarrassing prodigals, there is

hope. Hope was gone for Ruth Ann, though. Her prodigal would never come home.

Alcoholism, drug addition, crimes, and so much more characterize embarrassing prodigals. If you are not careful, embarrassment can make matters worse. Prodigals can manipulate and shame you into doing what they desire. If this is your type of prodigal, note it. You will need divine strength to get you through the days ahead. Yet you will make it! There is hope.

DEFIANT PRODIGALS

Many embarrassing prodigals are making choices they don't want to make. Many times they love their parents and their families. Defiant prodigals, on the other hand, are prodigals with a motive. They intend to hurt their families, especially their parents. They openly denounce the faith and moral standards of their childhood.

Several years ago, a bright Cindy arrived on a major college campus. She was a committed Christian. She was a sweet girl with a beautiful smile, and her parents delighted in her achievements.

In her junior year Cindy started dating a controlling and domineering young man. He wanted to drive a wedge between her and her parents. He especially wanted her to forsake her faith.

As graduation neared, Cindy's parents noticed a change

in her personality. Instead of the sweet Christian girl they loved, she became withdrawn. Her smile disappeared. Maybe, her parents thought, it was the transition from being a college student to becoming an employee. Phone calls were fewer, and when they came they lasted only a few moments. Something was wrong.

Job offers came, but she declined them. Cindy finally told her parents she was moving into her boyfriend's apartment. Reasoning with her failed. After listening to her controlling boyfriend for months, she concluded her parents were the cause of all her problems.

Cindy became angry and defensive. Her relationship with her parents deteriorated to a shallow politeness, at best.

As they feared, she became pregnant. Her boyfriend demanded that she get an abortion. Again, her parents tried to reason with her. In a rage, she verbally exploded. "You can't tell me what to do!" she yelled. "I'm on my own now, and I'll do whatever I want!"

Surprisingly, she chose to give birth. Her boyfriend left, claiming he was not sure that he was the father. Unbroken, the sweet, gentle girl who went to college now is an angry, defiant, unwed mother.

In a similar story, my wife, Debbie, and I know a middle-aged woman who helped us see the anger of another defiant prodigal. As a teenage girl, Whitney got sexually involved with a man. She became pregnant. Fortunately, the man agreed to marry her and care for the baby. A few years later, Whitney gave birth to another child. Their marriage, however, was never strong. She eventually divorced her husband, and she and her daughters lived alone for many years.

Loneliness was too painful to endure. Whitney met a man who was gentle and kind. He was a few years older, but he gave her the security she needed. But there was a problem. He was a convicted felon. His crime involved another family member. She knew her family would despise him.

Before the wedding, several friends and family members tried to get Whitney to change her mind, but she insisted on marrying him. Her family's resentment toward her and her decision to marry was so intense that most of her relatives refused to talk to her.

Debbie and I know Whitney well. We reached out to her. Amazingly, she was very open about her upcoming marriage. As she talked, we listened. We intentionally avoided any condemnation in our comments. We wished her well and assured her of our prayers. I discovered later our reaction surprised Whitney. She fully expected us to condemn her. Instead, we offered her grace.

As we talked, I realized the reason she wanted to marry this man. Whitney wanted to hurt the people who had hurt her. The divorce from her first husband was very embarrassing. Her parents and some family members said very unkind things to her. In fact, most of her family condemned her viciously.

The pain of condemnation she felt during her divorce drove her emotions. Whitney wanted to punish the family for her pain. Her method of retaliation was to marry a man they despised.

INTELLECTUAL PRODIGALS

The prodigal in your family might not fit those first two categories. Your prodigal does not engage in public sin. He obeys the law. She may be successful in her professional career. Your prodigal might be a wonderful, honorable person with no moral flaws—a good son or daughter, father or mother, husband or wife.

Many prodigals are not embarrassing to their families. Defiance is not their nature. Yet their hearts are far from God.

I call this group the intellectual prodigals. They are men and women who have abandoned their faith, who switched from a Christian outlook to a secular worldview. For them, nothing is certain. Everything is relative.

Growing up on the farm, Harry loved going to church. From his earliest days, he studied the Bible. His knowledge of the Scriptures rivaled most adults twice his age.

His parents knew the value of education. They determined their children would be college graduates. They lived modestly and saved every penny they could. Finally the day came when Harry, their oldest, became the first person in their families to leave for college.

On campus, professors soon challenged Harry's beliefs with humanistic concepts. He listened as biology professors scoffed at the idea of a Creator. Life is the result of coincidences, they said. Gradually, doubts eroded his faith.

With his undergraduate degree in hand, Harry applied for medical school. The school accepted his application. For the next few years, Harry devoted himself to his studies. By the time he graduated from medical school, Harry had no faith at all.

Harry, gifted with a brilliant mind, advanced in his profession. Before he was forty, he became the director of a research center at a leading hospital. Today, this renowned doctor never attends church, though the kindness and gentleness that characterized his childhood is there still.

Harry remains a friend. Occasionally we have tough conversations. Although I am no match for his intellect, we talk honestly about a Christian worldview. Harry has some doubts he cannot overcome, doubts placed there by secular professors. Unfortunately, no one helped him work through those challenges that hit him hard as a young undergrad student.

Harry experienced a personal and emotional blow as well. Doctors diagnosed his mother, a committed Christian, with cancer. For months, he watched helplessly as she wasted away. Harry heard the prayers of her friends. He heard his mother plead with the Lord for relief from her suffering. As a medical professional, Harry knew there was nothing doctors could do to help his mother. The death of Harry's mother validated, in his mind, that the secularists were right. Harry concluded that God does not exist.

Intellectual prodigals often begin questioning Christianity on a rational basis. Then a disappointment crushes what faith remains. They want evidence, proof that satisfies their logic.

Most family members, especially if they lack equivalent education, recoil from talking with intellectual prodigals. Moms and dads feel powerless. Hope vanishes. That is, hope vanishes until an intellectual prodigal encounters what science cannot provide—genuine love evidenced in a joy-filled life.

Huntsville, Alabama, is home to some of the greatest minds in the world. Most work for NASA or contractors related to NASA. Among their achievements is the *Saturn V* rocket that put man on the moon.

A few years ago I met Greg. Greg leads a team of engineers involved in designing rockets for future space travel. A former atheist, Greg today is a committed Christian. He and his family are very active in their church.

Greg, like most intellectual prodigals, knew about God.

As a child, his parents occasionally attended religious services. While a student pursuing his PhD, Greg abandoned any thought of God. For his engineering mind, religion was a creation by men. It was man's way of explaining what he did not understand.

Greg purchased a farm outside of Huntsville and moved his family there. Every day at work he explored complex theories. After a day of managing projects and leading a team, Greg enjoyed coming home to do farmwork. It was a hobby that provided needed stress relief.

The tractor Greg owned broke down regularly. One day he asked his elderly neighbor, George, to help him fix it. With time, George became a regular visitor to help Greg. They became dear friends.

George and Greg, however, were drastically different from one another. George could not read or write. Greg had a doctorate. George farmed all day, working with his hands. Greg sat at a desk, thinking about the ideas before him. George saw life as a blessing. Greg saw life as a competitive world where everyone thought only of himself or herself.

Every time George repaired a piece of equipment for Greg, the scientist insisted that George accept payment. The uneducated farmer always refused, saying only, "No, that's okay. I did it unto the Lord."

This illiterate old man was wise. He knew the condition of Greg's heart. He saw through the intellectual shell.

George saw an empty, troubled heart. George knew Greg lacked the answers to life's deepest questions.

After months of building the relationship and many tractor repairs, the farmer tearfully told the scientist, "You're a lot smarter than I am, but I sure wish you knew my Lord." Greg never responded. The kindness of the illiterate farmer did not warrant an argument.

Months passed. The two men often discussed the weather, the price of hay, and the best fertilizer to use. Repairing equipment became a regular activity together.

One day Greg's daughter became seriously ill. For the first time in his life, Greg began to think about the possibility of life after death. The scientist remembered an earlier conversation with George. He recalled George's brother being ill and dying. As Greg struggled emotionally with his daughter's illness, he asked the old farmer about his brother's death.

George recalled the long, painful death his brother endured. George, however, was not bitter. Greg was unable to keep his thoughts to himself. He finally asked George, "How can you believe in a God who let something like that happen to your brother?"

The old farmer looked at him gently and replied, "Yes, my brother died. And yes, in some ways it was tragic. But you don't understand. The Lord walked him through that pain, and I know I'm going to see my brother again someday.

That's what gives me hope." The simple faith of an illiterate farmer touched the heart of this brilliant scientist. A few days later Greg placed his trust in Christ.

George did not preach to Greg. He did not argue or rebuke him for his unbelief. At the same time, the intelligence of the scientist did not awe the farmer. George looked into Greg's heart and saw a lost and lonely man. Greg needed a friend and a Savior. Thanks to a faithful farmer who understood intellectual prodigals, the scientist received both.

Love conquers all, including the heart of an intellectual prodigal.

COMPLACENT PRODIGALS

Complacent prodigals, I believe, are the most common type of prodigal. They say the right words. They rarely argue. Most agree with you about the condition of their spiritual life. These prodigals are not opposed to Christianity. In fact, they will tell you that it is the right thing to do. Yet they lack motivation to live it.

For many complacent prodigals, their lukewarm attitude affects other areas of their life. Often they are not motivated to seek a job. Few devote themselves to their education. There are exceptions, of course. The one trait of all complacent prodigals is the lack of interest in spiritual matters.

When someone mentions this type of prodigal, I think of my friend Jim. He attends church on special occasions, but his heart is not in it. His father tries to shame Jim to get him involved. He tells Jim things like, "I told others you would be there, so don't let me down, son." On one occasion, the father tried to pressure Jim by volunteering him for a task at church. Needless to say, it did not work. Manipulation never motivates prodigals.

Jim shared with me his deepest feelings about church. He told me, "When I was young, I went to Sunday school and church. We never missed. My parents were leaders in the church, so Dad always had a meeting Sunday night and sometimes on Thursday night. Mom was part of a group that met every Monday night. Honestly, I felt robbed because the church stole my parents' attention from me."

His words were a revelation. Knowing his parents as I do, I knew they had no idea how Jim felt. He acknowledges his need for spirituality, but he feels it should be down the list of priorities. He added, "I'm not going to deny my kids the opportunity to be with me. I have to work six days a week, and I work late many nights. I don't get to see my wife and kids that often. Sunday morning is one of the best—and only—times for me to spend with them. That's why I don't go to church that often."

Jim's parents equate church attendance with spirituality. To them, it is one and the same. Jim believes spirituality is separate from church attendance. Both think they are right. Both are unwilling to budge on their beliefs.

Complacent prodigals fail to see that inconsistent church attendance may be a reflection of an undisciplined life. They certainly do not see church involvement as a reflection of their faith. Although church attendance doesn't automatically equate to spirituality, the more you go the more you'll grow. Jim needed to see that faith in God is a relationship. It is a relationship that permeates every area of our lives, including our family time. It is not a checklist of activities to prove your spirituality.

RELIGIOUS PRODIGALS

Another type of prodigal is concerning more families than ever. At first glance, they appear to be the loved ones who went the opposite direction. They are religious and committed. Unfortunately, they embrace a religion far from orthodox Christianity. Many of you know what I mean.

Just as parents and grandparents grieve when their children join a cult, family members are stunned when these prodigal brothers and sisters abandon their lives for the sake of a destructive ideology. Worse, family members watch in fear as their loved ones follow a psychologically deranged leader.

Mary comes to my mind when I think of religious prodigals. Her parents are friends of mine. When their children were living at home, they welcomed questions about the Christian faith. They often talked about other religions. Their goal was to help their children see the differences in faiths. Truth, the parents thought, always wins in the end.

When Mary went to college, her parents felt she would find a committed Christian man to marry. A few months after arriving, Mary started telling her parents about a guy she met. He was, she reported, the most wonderful person in the world. An opportunity presented itself for her parents to meet him. They, too, were impressed. Jerome was kind and respectful.

One afternoon, when Mary was home for Christmas break, she talked with her parents. She told them that Jerome belonged to a Bible study group. At first, the news delighted them. Later, Mary asked her father to look at the Bible study guide being used in the group, which was led by a local man in the college town. She knew what it contained.

This group taught that possessions were sinful and that communal living was the biblical standard. Sex was a community activity and a reward for being faithful to the teachings of the group. Mary's father could not believe what he was reading. A quick search on the Internet revealed his worst nightmares. The cult was an extreme group that saw women as sex slaves.

Adding to Mary's confusion during this time was seeing the church of her childhood experiencing controversy. Arguments occurred among leaders. During one meeting of the leadership, a sheriff's deputy had to keep order. The cult leader told Mary that this confirmed her parents' church was satanic.

Mary's parents are older now. Today, communication with Mary is rare. As far as her parents know, Mary is healthy. They know she is alive but little more.

Cults often provide the security people crave. A leader, regardless of how mentally ill he or she is, makes all the decisions. Before long, an attendee loses all sense of self-worth.

Churches, on the other hand, often become rigid and judgmental. Religious prodigals walk away because there is no place for sinners. Alcoholics cannot sit next to pious members. Older ladies look down their noses at a black man walking in with a white woman. Men see tattoos as a sign of drug addiction.

It is important for us to examine our hearts. Before we judge those who judge others, we must look at ourselves. What if an unmarried woman with three children, all with different fathers, walks into our church? Is she welcomed? Or does she face the scowl of self-righteousness? What about a man convicted of child abuse desperately seeking help?

Many churches have a sign for all to read. It is not on the door. It is on the faces of the congregation: "No prodigals allowed." Sadly, some parents hang a similar sign on their faces too.

Jesus told the story of the prodigal son in front of the self-righteous Pharisees, who taught that God did not allow prodigals into His kingdom. Jesus said He did.

There is someone standing at the door of your church and your house. Who is it? Is it a loving Father or is it a condemning Pharisee? Before you answer, your response to your prodigal might give you a clue.

- -

TRUTH TO REMEMBER

Having a loving heart opens the door for change, but a condemning spirit will lock it shut.

- -

Chapter 3

· · · — — · · ·

RESPONDING
TO YOUR PRODIGAL

EMBARRASSING PRODIGALS fill us with shame. We ignore them. We demand they accept responsibility for their actions. We pray. We hope for a change.

We respond to *defiant prodigals* with our own defiance. Their selfishness infuriates us. We match their foolishness with foolish words of our own. We match them yell for yell.

Intellectual prodigals may, on the surface, give us pride. Privately, though, we try to argue them back into the kingdom of God. We buy them scholarly books with a Christian worldview as gifts.

Complacent prodigals frustrate us. They know better. We try every method imaginable to motivate them. Nagging becomes our favorite pastime when we are together.

With *religious prodigals*, we may resort to dramatic measures to rescue our loved ones.

Everyone agrees the actions of our prodigals are not

appropriate. Most of us, though, are reacting instead of acting. We empower our prodigals by allowing them to control our actions. We do not see it that way, but they are.

In chapters 4 through 9, we will look at the six principles to help bring your son or daughter back to God, but first we must stop our destructive reactions. Before we can start making things better, we must stop making things worse.

CONDEMNATION

Our motives may be pure. Our intentions may be good. We want to bring our prodigals back to their faith in God, but our words often send a different message. Inwardly we are angry—angry with our prodigals for making foolish decisions. Angry at them for making us look like failures as parents.

So we express our anger through criticism and condemnation. We justify ourselves by seeing our prodigals' behavior as a terrible example. Our verbal stance against their sins, we think, is taking a stand for God and righteousness. You see, we want our prodigals to be a warning to others.

Condemnation is hard to see in our words. We do it because condemning someone who is sinning just feels right.

GUILT

The anger we feel, though, often can turn inward. Instead of condemning the prodigals, we condemn ourselves. Guilt grips us. We blame them for inappropriate behavior. We blame ourselves for poor parenting skills.

Guilt enables prodigals to manipulate their parents. After years of irresponsible behavior, parents still will wonder whether they should trust their child. After all, they feel it is their fault.

IGNORING THE PROBLEM

For some parents, the pain of facing reality is overwhelming; therefore, they do not face it at all. Parents refuse to think about their prodigals. This problem compounds itself when one family member faces reality and another denies it.

I recently listened to two parents arguing about their child who is an alcoholic. The father told me, "Our Chad has a huge problem with drinking. He's an alcoholic." The mother was not able to admit it. She shot back in anger at her husband, "How can you say that? Just because he drinks a beer or two doesn't make him an alcoholic!"

The husband then recounted the list of employers who had fired Chad. He mentioned his three failed marriages. Looking into his wife's eyes, he said, "Don't deny, Marge. You remember the many times we couldn't find him for days because he was drunk in some cheap motel."

Any objective person knows these are all irrefutable signs of a binge drinker. Still, the mother clung to her illusion. "He was just looking for another job. That's all."

Family members who ignore problems make excuses. They say, "Oh, he can't help it. He had such a difficult childhood." They often list a litany of hard times the child faced. They refuse to see his or her sin. It is easier to excuse prodigals than to hold them responsible for their actions.

LIES AND COVER-UPS

Most of the time we do not tell blatant lies about our prodigals. We just shade the truth to make the situation look better than it is. (Do you remember the father of the chaingang prisoner who said his son was working for the state?)

We blame failed marriages on sons-in-law or daughters-in-law. We paint rosy pictures of kids looking for better jobs, but neglect to say it is because their former boss fired them for looking at online porn sites while at work.

The truth, we fear, makes us look like bad parents. We fear our friends seeing us as failures. Family members often shade the truth so they can protect the reputation of their prodigals. In actuality, they are protecting their own reputation.

NAGGING

Your loved one is messing up her life, and you know exactly how to fix it. So you tell her. You tell her how to be a better parent, spouse, employee, and Christian. And you repeat it over and over, hoping repetition will help you get through to them. Your prodigal smiles and nods at you, but she's tuned you out a long time ago.

Some of us use spiritual threats to nag our children. We shake our heads and tell them they are going to suffer the fires of hell if they do not change their ways. We repeatedly warn them that they will reap what they sow. We think we are encouraging them. We believe we are calling them to righteousness. We convince ourselves that our words and actions are in our prodigals' best interests.

We nag because we know they can have a better life. Though they refuse to listen, nagging makes us feel as if we are doing something to change their ways.

FIXING THE PROBLEM

Many family members go beyond nagging to active involvement. They cannot watch their loved ones ruin their lives. So they think the problem needs fixing. This may be appropriate when our sons and daughters are in grade school. As an adult, though, prodigals need to take responsibility for their actions.

Let me illustrate.

John has an addiction to gambling. Over the years, he gambled thousands of dollars and lost every cent. When bookies came to collect, his parents wrote a check to make them go away. When the son wanted to make money in online stock trading, they gave him a loan to get started.

When the brokerage firm demanded payment for the huge debts from margined stocks, the parents paid again. Scores of times they warned him, "This is the last time we're going to give you any money." The last time never came. They always wrote the check.

Fixers believe they are doing the right thing. They believe removing the problem fixes the prodigal. Guilt and fear are powerful motivators to keep fixers doing whatever the prodigal wants. But fixing an irresponsible person's predicament prevents him from facing reality. Ultimately, it feeds the problem and prevents the brokenness that may lead to restoration.

QUIET ANGUISH

Some family members are tired. They've received advice, and they have given it. They quoted scriptures and prayed diligently. They no longer live with the dream that their loved ones will come to their senses. To them, the road always will be empty. Despair replaced their hope long ago.

Now disappointment prevents them from believing a miracle can happen. They feel alone. They feel abandoned by their prodigals, their friends, and their church. Does that sound like you? Do you feel hopeless? If so, I want to give you hope again. Change is possible.

In the past, we probably handled our prodigals the wrong way. They needed love, but we gave them shame.

They needed understanding, yet we gave them demands. They needed tough love, but we removed the consequences of their decisions.

So, if change is going to come, where will it begin? It must begin with us, not with the prodigals. Instead of trying to change them, we need God to change us.

I remember that night in Missouri when I cried out to God. I recall the names I listed and then contacted when I arrived home. I still hear the echoes of the prodigals from my interviews. More importantly, I see the actions of the father in the story of the prodigal son that Jesus told. From those moments, I discovered the principles I am going to share with you.

You need to prepare your heart. You are going to change. When you do, you will see the change in your prodigal.

- -

TRUTH TO REMEMBER

Your response to your prodigal often determines his or her response to you. Change, then, begins with you.

- -

Chapter 4

. . . — — . . .

PRINCIPLE ONE: GETTING OVER THE GUILT

"WHAT DID I DO WRONG?"

This haunting question echoes hundreds of times in conversations I have with parents. It is human nature for us to assign blame. Determining responsibility can be helpful if it leads to forgiveness and healing. But if condemnation is the only outcome, our analysis is destructive.

Compassion truly motivates some parents as they seek a solution and try to help the ones they love. If they can unmask the problems, they can address them forcefully and clearly. But far too many other parents are consumed with guilt rather than compassion. They believe the long, bony finger of blame points back at them. They are disillusioned under the tremendous weight of responsibility they feel for their children's problems.

You may recall me saying earlier that guilt allows the prodigal to manipulate a parent. Until you deal with the guilt you feel, you will be in a weak position to help your prodigal. And it is my experience that you can't deal with the guilt until you answer, "What did I do wrong?"

Surprisingly, my research revealed the answer. Every prodigal I interviewed gave me the same answer. But before I give it to you, you must understand why you feel responsible for the sin of your child. Based on what I discovered through my research, I'm confident that you basically feel guilty for two reasons: First, you have neglected the fact that your child has a sin nature, which affects his or her choices. Second, you believe, based on an incorrect interpretation of Scripture, that poor parenting caused wrong behavior.

Let's begin by looking at the first one.

OUR CHILDREN ARE SINNERS

Paul told the Roman believers, "For all have sinned and fall short of the glory of God" (Rom. 3:23). Theologians speak of this as "the depravity of man." That means we are fallen, sinful people from birth. We don't have to teach people to sin. They will do it naturally.

The Bible is full of instructions and admonitions to guide our choices. Paul typically used half of each of his letters to the churches to describe the glorious truths about our identity in Christ, and he used the other half to instruct us how that identity should be expressed in our choices. For example, in his letter to the Ephesians, he first described how God calls us: we are chosen by God, adopted, loved, and forgiven. Then he turned to application of those truths: "I, therefore, the prisoner of the Lord, beseech you to walk worthy of the calling with which you were called" (4:1). After this transition to the second half of the letter, he encouraged us to follow commands such as:

- don't lie, but speak the truth;
- don't steal, but give to those in need;
- don't be bitter, but forgive;
- don't destroy people with your words, but speak words that build people up.

Obviously, Paul provided these clear commands because we have a tendency to lie, steal, harbor bitterness, and use our words to hurt people. In other words, we have a propensity to sin.

Your prodigal has choices too. When a person becomes an adult, he is responsible for his own behavior: his choices, his attitudes, and his actions. He may act like a selfish, spoiled child, but God will hold him accountable as an adult.

Someone may have suffered terribly as a child, and her life may be colored by many tragic experiences, but she is still accountable for her own choices.

Because of the nature to choose sin, perfect parenting cannot guarantee a godly child.

In Jesus' parable of the prodigal son, what sins do we see the father commit? None! What did he do to alienate his son and drive him away from home? Nothing! It's simply not in the story. He was a good parent. Still, his son chose to reject his father's company in pursuit of harmful pursuits.

The Bible provides several examples of people who made bad choices even after they enjoyed a good environment. Jesus spent three years with His twelve disciples. He never sinned. He always showed them perfect love, yet Judas betrayed Him for thirty pieces of silver, and the rest of the disciples ran during His moment of greatest need.

What did Jesus do wrong with His disciples? Nothing!

Adam and Eve lived in the perfection of the garden of Eden, with everything they could possibly want. They chose to sin against God. They thought rebellion was better than obedience. Before that day, they had never known evil. But since that day, evil has been present in the world.

What did God do wrong with Adam and Eve? Nothing!

The children of Israel were rescued from slavery in Egypt. Miracles marked the beginning of their journey, and miracles sustained them day after day. But they grumbled and complained so often that God let that first generation die in the desert instead of allowing them to enter the Promised Land.

What did God do wrong with the Israelites? Nothing!

In the early church, Paul discipled a man named Demas. At first, he was a faithful follower who ministered alongside Paul and Luke. In his short letter to Philemon, Paul referred to Demas as "my fellow laborer" (v. 24). In Paul's eyes, Demas was a valued friend and co-laborer in the cause of Christ. But in a later letter to Timothy, Paul reported sadly, "For Demas has forsaken me, having loved this present world, and has departed for Thessalonica" (2 Tim. 4:10). Demas enjoyed the encouragement and the example of the apostle Paul, one of the greatest Christians in all of history, yet he chose to become a prodigal. He left Paul because he wanted comfort and wealth.

What did Paul do wrong? Nothing!

Each of these examples depicts someone who was loved and valued deeply, by Jesus personally, by God in the garden and in the wilderness, or by the apostle Paul. But in each case, perfect love failed to keep those people from becoming prodigals. They made their own choices to turn away from God.

So the first point I want to make—and make it clearly—is your prodigal is bent toward sin. If he does what is "natural" for him to do, he will choose to be a prodigal. But with that choice comes a responsibility. Your prodigal is responsible for his choices.

"DOESN'T THE BIBLE BLAME ME?"

You may be able to accept that truth. But doesn't the Bible share some of the blame with you, as a parent? That question leads us to the second source of guilt in parents of prodigals.

One of the most common laments I've heard from parents is, "Doesn't the Bible teach that if I'd been a better parent, my child would be walking with the Lord today?"

In most cases, they refer to Proverbs 22:6, which has been a source of tremendous guilt and confusion for parents of prodigals. It reads:

Train up a child in the way he should go,
And when he is old he will not depart from it.

Many people look at this verse as a promise rather than a proverb. Promises are always true; proverbs are generally true but not always. For example, another proverb says that a man who sleeps with harlots will lose his wealth. While it is true that sexual sins often cost people a lot of money, I know some men who regularly visit prostitutes but are still very rich.

Other scholars take a different approach to this verse. They believe it means to instruct a child on his level so he will understand the truth. For example, you wouldn't use Greek words in teaching a five-year-old Sunday school class. If so, they would never remember what you said.

Others say that the phrase "in the way he should go" refers to a child's "bent." That is, parents should notice each child's particular gifts, skills, and personality and then give encouragement and direction based on those traits. So a child who is gifted in art could be given lessons in painting and sculpting; a child who is athletically talented should be given opportunities to play sports; and a child who is good at math is encouraged to pursue more challenging course work in algebra and calculus.

This interpretation makes good sense to me. I think parents are right in observing and nurturing the particular skills of each of their children. Yet as I have studied this passage of Scripture, I believe there is another meaning for us to consider.

Psychologists tell us that childhood profoundly shapes our lives. How we are reared affects us for the rest of our lives, for good or ill. If a child is told she is fat and ugly, she probably will be insecure about her appearance as an adult. If a child is abused or neglected, those scars will make him cautious in relationships even after being placed in a safe environment. If a child is constantly nagged and criticized, he will doubt his abilities.

These are the negative aspects we usually tend to focus on, but there is also a positive side to the same principle. If a child is exposed to the ways and the truth of God when he is young, those messages will stay in his heart for the rest of his life. Though his choices and behavior may take him far from God, the truth of God stays lodged in his mind.

Proverbs 22:6 doesn't promise that a child will never depart from God's path; instead, it reminds us that God's message remains rooted in that person's life and cannot be eradicated. It always will be a silent conviction in his or her life.

Do you remember what happened to the prodigal son? He had gone as far away from his father as he could go. He was feeding hogs in a foreign land, penniless and friend-less. But even there he remembered his father's goodness and strength. The childhood memories of his father's love prompted a desire to return to his dad as he realized he might be extended the grace to repent and come home.

The example and the teachings of his father never left his heart.

Nowhere in Scripture does it say that if you had just done the right thing as a parent, your child would be walking with God today. No, the Scriptures teach two important lessons: (1) Each person has the tendency to choose sin, and (2) If your child was exposed to the Bible, that truth is still there to be tapped by the Holy Spirit whenever your child "comes to himself." These two lessons help us clarify responsibility so we can be relieved of guilt.

So, now let me answer the original question: What did I do wrong?

The answer? Probably nothing!

You can spend the rest of your life analyzing every moment of a prodigal's life and never find a reason. Only guilt will occur. And guilt, you remember, weakens your ability to help your prodigal. Until the Holy Spirit tells you differently, you must assume you did nothing wrong as a parent to cause your child to walk away.

THE BLAME GAME

If we as family members aren't to blame, then who is? Human nature demands that somebody take the blame when things go wrong. Many times we blame ourselves. Other times we blast away at somebody else.

One of the most common people to blame for a child's waywardness is a student pastor. "If the youth director had just called one more time, Roy would have gone to church camp that summer instead of starting to smoke marijuana and eventually becoming a drug addict."

Parents often do mental and emotional gymnastics in order to place blame on somebody or some situation. "Judy's biology teacher spent so much time talking about reproduction, I just know that's what got Judy interested in sex. She got pregnant, and it's that biology teacher's fault." (As if Judy wouldn't have been interested in sex had she not learned about the reproductive habits of frogs!)

Sometimes family members desperately search for a

situation from the past that will magically explain why their child has become a prodigal. "My son and his best friend were riding their bikes when they were nine years old. A car hit Jeff's friend, and he almost died as result. I just know Jeff has never been the same since then. He became an alcoholic and has gone through four divorces, but it all goes back to that day when his best friend got run over."

As outside observers, we can see the irrational conclusions of these parents. But if we were able to be objective about ourselves, we would agree that we have irrational thoughts in certain areas of our lives as well.

Several years ago I met Bob, an elderly gentleman in a church where I spoke. His son had caused him and his wife a lot of pain. Bob told me the heartbreaking story of how his son was molested by the assistant pastor of their church years ago. "My boy's not in church today," he related sadly. "I'm sure that terrible experience is what drove him away from church."

Let me be clear: the molestation that took place was in no way his son's fault. Fortunately, the perpetrator was arrested, convicted, and sentenced to prison. I know the horrible actions of the molester had serious, negative effects on the young man.

I shared with Bob that many victims of sexual abuse and other kinds of terrible sins are experiencing healing and hope. Their relationship with our Lord is strong. Sadly, Bob refused to accept that possibility. He, too, lost hope and found his only satisfaction by blaming rather than trying to work with his son to bring about healing.

COMPARISON KILLS

Many parents are proud of their children, and rightly so. They love to tell everyone who will listen about their son's successful business or their daughter's recent mission trip.

When family members of prodigals hear these stories, it is like salt being poured into their wounds. Instead of being encouraged, they feel self-doubt and discouragement all over again. In fact, their pain feels more severe when contrasted with someone else's joy.

To the parents or grandparents of a prodigal, sometimes the loudest words are those unspoken. They hear in the joy of the family members of the faithful: *If you were as spiritual as I am, your child would be doing well too.*

As a result, parents of prodigals play the "if only" game. They speculate:

- "If only I'd had a better job like Sam Johnson, then I would have made enough so my Mary could have gone to a better school and not gotten into trouble."
- "If only my husband hadn't died. My son needed a stronger hand to guide him."

- "If only we'd taken more time for vacations, my kids would care about us more now that we're older."
- "If only we'd gone to a different church, my son would have gotten better teaching about walking with God. His life would be different today."

Parents think of a thousand "if onlys" and "what-ifs." None of them, however, soothe the pain. The thoughts only redirect the blame to themselves. Family members are powerless to change the past, and they feel helpless to change the present. So they continue to live every day feeling ashamed, guilty, and hopeless.

"I GUESS I'LL JUST HIDE"

Guilt crushes us from the inside. It drains the joy out of life and leaves us lonely, bitter, and discouraged.

Many family members of prodigals, especially parents, have lived with guilt for so long that they have adopted three "rules" of painful families:

1. Don't talk to anyone.
2. Don't trust anyone.
3. Don't feel anything.

They talk about everything except the pain they feel. They may even ask for prayer for their prodigal. But when somebody asks, "How are you doing with all this?" they smile and say, "Oh, I'm fine. Don't worry about me." They are dying inside, though, and don't want anybody to know it.

Parents who have been repeatedly disappointed grow disillusioned. They give up hope for a meaningful relationship, one based on trust, with their wayward sons or daughters. Instead, they talk only about surface things and avoid mentioning topics that are painful—or important.

Disappointment can color our own relationships with God when we love a prodigal. We hope and pray, but nothing changes. Our trust in God starts to vanish. We stop seeking joy in life. Our goal is only to avoid any more pain.

The result is a world of numbness where hurts are not as intense. But neither is joy. Depression often comes. Sometimes the depression becomes clinical depression. It often occurs gradually. Then something triggers it. It might be an explosive fight with the prodigal. Maybe your son is in trouble with the law again. Or she is going through another divorce. Soon *any* joy in life eludes us. Things that once made us happy become tedious. Friends become a nuisance. We sleep too much or not at all. Eating seems like too much trouble, or we eat constantly. Don't talk, don't trust, and don't feel.

These sinister "rules" become the norm for parents of prodigals if they don't relieve their guilt with peace, forgiveness, and joy.

WHAT NOW?

So, have you been playing the blame game in your mind—blaming yourself, someone else, or circumstances? Or have others, friends and family members, been blaming you for the path your prodigal is on? It's time to stop this negative thinking.

Blaming yourself only brings guilt. Guilt, in turn, allows the prodigal to control your relationship. You become powerless to help.

Blaming others only brings bitterness. Bitterness, then, causes you to die from within and allows anger to fill your heart where joy once strived.

True, you may think you nagged too much, worked too many hours, or spoiled your kids with money and possessions. Maybe you overprotected your children and didn't allow them to make their own decisions. If you still struggle thinking you did something wrong with the prodigal in your family, will you allow the Holy Spirit to settle it?

God gave us a conscience to show us our faults. But our conscience sometimes looks for faults that do not exist. The Bible, on the other hand, encourages believers to listen to the Holy Spirit when we are uncertain whether our actions have been sinful or wrong. Sometimes our human conscience may be blaming us, piling guilt upon guilt on our heavy hearts, when the Holy Spirit is trying to restore our joy.

The Bible describes a huge difference between oppressive guilt and the conviction of the Holy Spirit. Conviction is the process of God getting me to acknowledge my sin if I am listening to Him. When I confess my sin, it is forgiven and I'm able to put it behind me.

A conscience looking for fault makes me feel bad, and guilt is accompanied by an inability to accept God's forgiveness. Conviction that results in repentance restores my joy. Guilt is backward thinking; conviction is forward thinking. Guilt makes us feel that if we punish ourselves severely enough and long enough, we can compensate for our faults. Conviction of the Holy Spirit brings peace so we can move on.

One time Paul discovered that the Corinthian believers were committing serious sins, so he wrote them a letter to challenge them to repent. To his delight, they responded to his instructions. When he learned of their response, he wrote:

> For even if I made you sorry with my letter, I do not regret it; though I did regret it. For I perceive that the same epistle made you sorry, though only for a while. Now I rejoice, not that you were made sorry, but that your sorrow led to repentance. For you were made sorry in a godly manner, that you might suffer loss from us in nothing. For godly sorrow produces

repentance leading to salvation, not to be regretted; but the sorrow of the world produces death. (2 Cor. 7:8–10)

"The sorrow of the world produces death." That's guilt. This death is the sense that we are helpless, hopeless, and worthless. It tells us there is no remedy to solve our problems. But in contrast, "godly sorrow produces repentance . . . not to be regretted." *Godly sorrow* is the conviction of the Holy Spirit. The result is no guilt.

When we experience God's cleansing grace for our sins, we celebrate forgiveness. Paul said it another way in his letter to the Romans: "There is therefore now no condemnation to those who are in Christ Jesus" (8:1). If you know Christ as your personal Savior, His grace covers all our sins. There is no condemnation anymore, only forgiveness. No more oppressive guilt, only grace. Let me outline some of the differences between destructive guilt and the positive conviction of the Holy Spirit.

- *Guilt tells you that you are worthless—that what you've done is so bad, nothing can ever overcome it.*
- The Holy Spirit's conviction tells us our behavior is wrong but that we are still loved by God.
- *Guilt makes us want to hide.*

- The Holy Spirit's conviction gives us courage to restore the relationships of those we have hurt.
- *Guilt focuses on others' opinions of us.*
- The Holy Spirit's conviction focuses on God's opinion of us, motivating us to please Him above all else.
- *Guilt produces fear.*
- The Holy Spirit's conviction produces joy.
- *Guilt makes us want to find someone else to blame.*
- The Holy Spirit's conviction leads to repentance, forgiveness, and refreshment so we don't feel compelled to blame anyone anymore.

We must use both reason and faith to move beyond any oppressive guilt we feel to experience the joy of being forgiven and loved by God. You must refuse to interpret your prodigal's behavior as an indictment of you. Others may believe that lie, but God doesn't. You undoubtedly did the best you knew how to do.

FINDING GRACE IN STRANGE PLACES

Recently, a couple in their midseventies asked to talk to me after I spoke at their church. Their daughter was divorced and remarried to a man about whom they had reservations. She retained custody of her nine-year-old daughter, who one day called her grandparents very upset. She asked if she could come visit. When she arrived, she was barely in the front door when she blurted out that her mother and new stepfather were dealing drugs.

The grandfather asked a few questions and found out more than he wanted to know. The young girl told him detailed facts about her parents' client list and suppliers. Her stepfather had a minimum-wage job, but he was driving a Jaguar. He wore expensive jewelry. All that money had to be coming from somewhere.

The grandparents feared for their daughter's life. In a greater way, their granddaughter's safety concerned them. They knew enough from reports on the local news to know that drug dealers are put in jail or, worse, sometimes killed when a drug deal goes bad. They went to a counselor for advice. He immediately advised them to go to the authorities, so they did, hoping they could plead for mercy.

At the police station, the grandfather learned that his son-in-law was already under surveillance. The police said they needed further information before they could arrest the couple. The grandfather went back home, got additional details from the little girl, and took the information to the police department. The police then arrested his daughter and son-in-law. Months later, they went to prison.

The trial revealed to the couple that the grandparents were the informants. They were irate and hired a lawyer to prevent the grandparents from seeing their granddaughter. Even though the parents went to jail, the court decided the grandparents would receive very limited visitation rights.

The grandfather told me, "Phil, I wish I'd never gone to the police. Ten thousand times I'd take it back. Now my daughter and son-in-law have nothing to do with me. They say they're going to kill us when they get out. I can only see my granddaughter for two hours a month now, and they say when they get out I'll never see her again. She will be a teenager then. I feel just awful because I didn't do the right thing."

The old gentleman's wife cried as he told their story. She, however, through her tears told me confidently, "Phil, I came to the conclusion that we did the right thing. I don't have guilt, because I have faith that when my granddaughter listens to the whole story, she'll know we acted in her best interest. I came to the conclusion, as painful as it is, that sometimes doing the right thing costs a lot."

This couple exemplifies two responses to a prodigal. The man feels guilt because he could not make his daughter walk with God. He failed to help her make good decisions about life. Her sin crushed him.

His wife, on the other hand, was a paragon of insight, grace, and strength. She refused to believe her daughter's lies and accusations. Instead, she held tightly to the truth and trusted that God would someday make it right.

She grieved deeply over the events involving her granddaughter, but her grief didn't cloud the truth. She is an example for anyone with a prodigal.

At this point you may be saying, "But, Phil, the issue is not with me and God. It is with the prodigal. I feel as though there is something there—something between us—and I don't know what it is!" Then principle two is for you.

- -

TRUTH TO REMEMBER

Your prodigal is responsible for his or her actions. You are not. Stop feeling guilty, or you will be powerless to help your prodigal.

- -

Chapter 5

· · · — — · · ·

PRINCIPLE TWO: REMOVING THE BARRIERS

CHANGE BEGINS TO HAPPEN when you ask the Holy Spirit to reveal your heart. When you do, you must be receptive to His voice. He may bring to your mind a mistake you made that erected a barrier between you and your son or daughter. Things like:

You had an affair.

You shamed or embarrassed your prodigal in front of family or friends.

You lost control and slapped him.

You were not there when she was crowned homecoming queen.

You screamed, "I wish you were never born!"

The list of possibilities goes on and on.

For others, you are not sure what the problem is. Something went wrong for sure, but you have no idea what it is. You just know your relationship with your prodigal feels cool and distant.

Larry recently told me about his grown, married son who has always been cool toward him. Larry first noticed a strain in the relationship when his son was in high school. He assumed, however, that it was a phase.

When the young man went to college, he rarely came home. During their times together, Larry's son was pleasant but superficial. When the father asked personal questions, his son gave quick answers and changed the subject. Clearly he did not want to reveal his feelings to his father.

Larry tried to rationalize this distance in their relationship. As time passed, Larry's rationalization turned to heartache. After his son got married, he noticed how free and relaxed his son seemed to be with his in-laws. The pain hurt, but he said nothing.

Larry's emotions went from a desire to talk to fearing what his son might say. On the one hand, they were not arguing and cursing each other. Their relationship was better than what most sons and fathers have. On the other hand, he knew a barrier existed between them.

After several more years, the pain had become unbearable. I suggested that he ask his son if there was anything that had caused the problem. At first, Larry protested, "If I did anything to hurt him, surely he would have said something by now, Phil. It's been years!"

"Or he may be wondering why you haven't said anything after all these years," I replied.

Larry nodded and promised to try.

When his son and family visited the next summer, he asked his son to join him on the back porch. There, he swallowed hard and said, "Son, this is hard for me. It seems there has been distance between us for some time. I can't think of any childhood event that would have hurt you, but there must be something. Please tell me what I've done to offend you."

The son took a deep breath. Tears welled up in his eyes, and he told his dad, "Yes, sir. You hurt me deeply when I was thirteen. Do you remember when I made the all-star baseball team that summer?"

His father nodded, "Yes, I was really proud of you."

"You were out of town for our first playoff game. I called and told you, 'Dad, we won! The championship game is Friday night. You'll be there, won't you?' But you said you couldn't make it."

Larry began to speak, but the son stopped him.

"Dad, that's not what hurt. But the next week, Charles [his dad's favorite nephew] called and asked you to go to his game. Dad, you took a day of vacation to go to his game, but you didn't go to mine. That's what really hurt."

Tears were flowing down his son's cheeks.

Larry was a surrogate father to his nephew because his sister was a single mom. He wanted to explain that Charles needed as much affirmation as possible. He had a good excuse. Wisely, though, he did not say those things. Instead of defending himself, he replied, "Son, I am so sorry. Please forgive me. Thank you so much for talking to me."

If Larry had defended himself, his son would have walked away with an even deeper wound. He did not. He just apologized.

That day marked a turning point in their relationship. The coolness gave way to warmth. Superficial conversation turned into deep, heartfelt communication. Larry regretted that he had not talked to his son twenty years earlier.

One honest conversation without excuses can remove barriers that exist.

Forgiveness is the cornerstone of our relationship with God. It ought to be the cornerstone of our human relationships as well. In fact, honesty with God about our sinfulness is a springboard for honesty in our other relationships. Those simple words, "I was wrong. Please forgive me," are incredibly powerful. They open doors of truth and grace in our relationships with those we love. Far too often, however, we are too proud to utter them.

TYPES OF WOUNDS

When we think about wounding our children, our thoughts drift to the extreme examples we hear about on the evening news:

"A mother locked her two children in the trunk of her car when she went shopping. One died and the other is in intensive care."

"A father killed his wife in a drunken rage in front of his children. Detectives are still trying to determine his motives."

These and similar stories horrify us. Granted, they leave deep wounds. But most of our wounds fail to make the evening news. They are common and hard to identify. I would put the types of hurts we experience, or inflict on others, in four categories: shattering wounds, eroding wounds, vacuum wounds, and spiritual wounds.

Shattering Wounds

Physical or sexual abuse shatters a child's heart and leaves him or her broken. Other traumatic experiences also are sledgehammers on a child's soul:

• the sudden and/or violent death of a parent,

- witnessing a parent physically abusing the other, or
- having a student pastor steal money from the church.

Although no one is prepared for these traumatic experiences, children and teenagers struggle to process them. In their innocent world, they do not make sense, so they often begin distrusting adults and questioning God.

Because they never share their pain, no one senses the need for a counselor or an adult to intervene. They hurt alone, and the hurt begins to change their outlook on people, life, and their self-worth.

When traumatic experiences create deep wounds that leave someone anger, bitter, or resentful, we often do not know how to address them. One family member tried to explain this type of wound by saying, "Well, I think my sister just needs to get over it."

Eroding Wounds

More common are the sandpaper effects of harsh, condemning messages. Words like:

"You'll never amount to anything!"

"Can't you do anything right?"

"Why don't you get out of here and leave me alone?"

"Why can't you be like your sister?"

Some of these messages are overcome with lots of love and repentance. Where there is no repentance, however, the wound festers.

In many cases, parents harshly corrected their children and justified it as necessary with a strong-willed child, but these parents gave precious little love and affirmation along with their correction. The result was harsh condemnation and shattered self-confidence.

Janice was eleven years old when her mother fell in love with another man and decided to leave her husband. Janice overheard her mother tell a neighbor, "I don't want my kids. I don't care if I never see them again!" Her mother moved out, planning to disappear without a trace.

A few days later, however, Janice's mother found out that her lover refused to leave his wife and marry her. In the aftermath of this event, God touched this mother's heart and she became a Christian. She came back home. Her husband forgave her. Life continued.

One day Janice reminded her mother of the penetrating, damaging words she had overheard. Her mother refused to discuss it, other than to tell her, "Oh, you know I was just kidding."

Janice's mother never apologized for her words. The family swept that episode under the rug and never talked about it. Her father once told Janice, "I've forgiven your mother for having an affair. Now she's home, and everything's the way it should be. We don't need to discuss it again."

But Janice retained a deep and painful emotional wound. The initial trauma gave way to the erosion caused by repeated messages that she wasn't important enough to warrant addressing the issue. When Janice was asked about it years later as an adult, she replied tartly, "I know how my mother feels about me." She completely detached from her mother and to this day maintains a very superficial relationship with the family.

In recent years, her mother has tried to reach out to her. The mom, however, still refuses to talk with Janice about the event that caused the pain. The last time Janice brought it up, her mother cut her off quickly with the comment, "That's ancient history, Janice. We need to live in the present. Just let it go." Janice walked out, hurt again that her mother was unwilling to even acknowledge her pain. After this brief exchange, her mother explained to her dad, "I didn't mean what I said that day. And besides, she was eavesdropping. I wouldn't have said it if I'd known she was listening. I wish she'd just drop it and get on with her life."

Janet experienced this tragic crisis at an age when little girls are close to their mothers. At that vulnerable moment in her life, her mother deeply wounded her. And she still is wounding her. A whole world of healing and hope might open up if this mother, who is now a Christian, would acknowledge that what she did was wrong and ask for Janice's forgiveness.

Vacuum Wounds

One of the wounds hardest to heal is neglect. Physical abuse leaves bruises. Verbal abuse is experienced through harsh words and scowling faces. Neglect is an altogether different type of abuse. We can experience an entire childhood of neglect without having a distinctive wound to identify or an evident loss to grieve—and instead only feel emptiness.

After talking to hundreds of young people over the years, I believe neglect is one of the most painful wounds to endure and one of the most difficult to heal.

Men often appear unfazed by the pain of others. Their parents taught them to "suck it up" when they felt hurt. They expect their children to do the same thing.

Vince Lombardi, the late legendary coach of the Green Bay Packers, was a man's man, a motivator, and someone who produced champions. He was tough, and he did not coddle his players. During one game, one of his guys blew out his ACL (a ligament in the knee) and was writhing on the field in pain. Lombardi walked over to him and barked, "Get up and get back in the game! You're not hurt!"

I have talked to some grown prodigals who feel this hard-hearted sentiment is a perfect description of their fathers' lack of compassion when they were hurting.

Spiritual Wounds

An extremely painful and confusing experience a child can undergo has been labeled "toxic faith." When physical or verbal offenses occur in a home, the child feels helpless. But when they take place in a home led by parents who profess to follow Christ, the child also feels terrified of God. It causes them to feel hopeless.

Too many people will not enter a church because of their father. Maybe he was an elder or deacon, but he was mean to them. One woman told me that her mom viciously spanked her if she failed to perfectly memorize her assigned Bible verses. In most of these cases, the parents have reputations in the community as paragons of Christian virtue. Family members fear exposing the lie and incurring even more wrath. They feel trapped.

Jill, a woman in her forties, told me that her father was a leader in their church. He taught Sunday school and served on several committees and boards. People saw him as a godly leader. Jill revered her father, but she felt little love from him. She told me,

> What my father said was the law around our house. He wouldn't tolerate anyone questioning his authority. Not at all. He read the Bible to us every night, but it seemed he loved the Old Testament best—you know, the stories about wars and God's judgment

on the people when they were disobedient. I can't remember him laughing and smiling around the house, and I can't remember him hugging me. When I was a little girl, I was terrified of him. I loved him dearly, but I was so afraid of him.

When I became a teenager, I was like any other adolescent. I wanted to wear the latest clothes and new hairstyles and hang out with friends, but Dad would have nothing of it. He told me I was being worldly, and he warned that I would go to hell if I didn't do what he said. I wish I had a nickel for every time he quoted Exodus 20:12: "Honor your father and your mother, that your days may be long upon the land which the LORD your God is giving you." It got to where I couldn't stand it anymore.

One night I went out drinking with some friends, and when I got home you'd have thought I had worshiped Satan or something. Dad came un-glued! He told me I had sinned against God and against him, and he was ashamed of me. He didn't speak to me for a month after that. And when he did start speaking to me again, I wished he hadn't.

I asked her, "Jill, where was your mother during all this?"

"Oh, she was right there," Jill said, her eyes widening. "She saw it all, but she was just as terrified of him as I was.

Sometimes, when Dad was really angry at me, she'd come in my room and say something like, 'Jill, it would be a lot easier around here if you'd just do what your father says. He'd be a lot happier.' I never saw my mother stand up to him. Not once."

"How did your relationship with your father affect your walk with God?" I probed.

"What relationship with God? I was just as terrified of God as I was of my father. I believed God was good and kind to other people, but I couldn't believe He loved me—not after all the verses about judgment my father quoted over and over again. And not after the way he treated me and my mother."

Jill thought for a moment, and then she continued.

It's been only in the last couple of years that I've begun to believe that God might actually love me. I've had a lot of healing to do, but gradually, with the help of some friends, it's happening. My dad is still just as distant and judgmental as he used to be, but I don't listen to him as I did when I was young. I still love my dad. I really do. But unless God does something drastic in his life, I know that this is the best relationship we're going to have. It's not much, but it's all he's willing to have. I'm certainly willing to take steps forward, and I've tried to let him know how I feel, but he doesn't want to talk about it. It's as if I'm speaking a foreign language or something. At least I can see that I'm a lot more loving toward my daughter than he was toward me.

The gospel of John tells us that Jesus came "full of grace and truth" (1:14). Children need truth, but they need grace just as much. It's not one or the other. Some parents meant well by giving their children rigid religious demands, using the Bible to justify their harsh punishments, but their actions only confused their children. As a result, prodigals often need kindness, understanding, and love.

THE REAL THING

The concept of forgiveness is clear throughout the pages of Scripture. In the Old Testament, God instructed the Israelites to follow elaborate temple rituals, including blood sacrifices for sins. They looked forward to a day when a perfect sacrifice would come. And He did. Jesus' death on the cross was the fulfillment of the Old Testament prophecies about the coming Messiah. Jesus was the "Lamb of God," who would take "away the sins of the world!" (John 1:29).

During His earthly ministry, Jesus taught and modeled forgiveness for His followers. Matthew 18 includes a parable about an unforgiving servant. This servant owed the king ten thousand talents. A talent was a unit of measurement, probably twenty to fifty pounds of a precious metal like silver or gold. In today's valuation of gold, the servant owed the king almost two billion dollars! Jesus obviously wanted to emphasize that this was an amount far more than the servant could ever hope to repay. Ordinarily, the government forced the debtor and his family to become indentured servants until the debt was repaid (in this case, for the rest of their lives). The king, however, felt compassion for the servant and released him from the debt. That was wonderful news . . . but that was only half of Jesus' story.

Earlier, that same servant had loaned a fellow servant a much smaller amount of money. But when the second servant was unable to repay his debt, the forgiven servant choked him and threw him into prison. Other servants told the king what the first servant did, which made the king furious.

The experience of forgiveness should have made a difference in the man's life. It should have made him more thankful and compassionate. He, however, failed to learn that lesson. Consequently, the king "was angry, and delivered him to the torturers until he should pay all that was due him" (v. 34). Jesus wanted His hearers to get the point. He explained that they must let God's forgiveness sink deep into their souls so it shapes their relationships. He told them, "So My heavenly Father also will do to you if each of you, from his heart, does not forgive his brother his trespasses" (v. 35).

Receiving and giving forgiveness doesn't come naturally to us—that's why we must learn how to do it from the great depth of God's forgiveness of us. If we have drunk deeply of God's great grace, we can be honest about our own sins. The cleansing flood of His forgiveness should make us more compassionate toward those who sin against us. If, however, we fail to appreciate God's grace, we become defensive and angry.

In a *Christianity Today* article many years ago, Philip Yancey wrote an article entitled "The Unnatural Act." The article said that people want to punish an offender (dispense justice) far more than they want to forgive him (show mercy). Forgiving someone, therefore, is "unnatural."

In the same way, asking someone for forgiveness is also "unnatural." We would much rather retreat than admit that we are wrong. Facing those we offended and confessing our faults takes great courage. It is the vital step in reconciliation if you want to reach your prodigal.

EXPLAINING DOESN'T WORK

Older family members, especially, only want to seek forgiveness when they are sure they were wrong. Even then, they are very hesitant.

Occasionally a family member plays the role of peacemaker. A prodigal says that her father did not pay enough attention to her. The father refuses to admit it. The family member jumps in the middle and says to the father, "Well, you did work two jobs when Alice was little, so she might have felt neglected."

He grumbles, "Yeah, but she doesn't appreciate all I did for her."

Then the family member pleads with the daughter, "He was doing all that for you. Please don't be angry."

Nothing changes. In fact, the situation grows worse. While the father makes excuses and the family member tries to make treaties, the prodigal continues to hurt. Explaining and excusing are no substitutes for forgiveness.

Many prodigals tell me something like, "When I was growing up, my dad worked ten hours a day, seven days a week. Dad didn't have time for my ball games or piano recitals." Parents accused of neglecting their children because they worked so hard almost invariably reply, "But you don't understand. I grew up in a very poor neighborhood. My parents could not read or write, so they never had jobs that offered us more than the bare necessities of life—and sometimes we didn't have that. I didn't have books to read. I cried because I didn't have toys to play with, and I vowed that my children would never suffer as I had."

This determination led them to work long hours to be sure their children were not hungry. The problem was that these children often went hungry for love.

Fifty years ago parents challenged children to be better

and do more. If a boy came home from school with straight As, a parent might remark, "That's pretty good," but would follow up with a sly smile and say, "I bet you can't do it again." Parents wanted to motivate their child to work hard, thinking, *We're challenging him to be the best he can be.* What the youngster heard was, "You'll never be able to please us completely." Parents thought they were helping. The child only felt disappointment.

TAKE THE INITIATIVE

Most family members avoid talking to prodigals about the strain in their family relationships. Most families go for years abiding by an unspoken truce. Some have told me, "If there was something wrong, she'd tell me. I don't want to stir up something that isn't there." So another year—or another decade—passes with no resolution. The bursts of anger are quickly swept under the rug instead of being seen for what they are: red flags that signal something is seriously wrong and needs attention.

Don't wait for your prodigal to take the first step. Take it yourself.

As you do, here are some areas to prepare for the time.

Ask God for Wisdom

At the close of one of the most beautiful psalms, King David asked God to show him every fault in his life. He did not want anything between him and the Lord in his life. He wanted God to point out any shortcomings so he could be cleansed of his sin and live in grace. David wrote:

Search me, O God, and know my heart;
Try me, and know my anxieties;
And see if there is any wicked way in me,
And lead me in the way everlasting.
(Ps. 139:23–24)

Your prodigal's response to you may be signaling that a barrier exists between you. Like David, ask for insight, and trust the Lord to provide wisdom. Ask God to remind you of events in the past that may have hurt your son or daughter. Let the Holy Spirit bring memories to mind. You may be surprised by what He reveals. If you still do not know what you did to hurt your prodigal, ask God to give you wisdom so you can ask your prodigal what is wrong.

Prepare Your Opening Statement and Question

If you know what you did to hurt your prodigal, you can begin by saying, "Son, there's something very important I want to talk to you about. I've been thinking about that time when you were in junior high and I [slapped you or yelled at you or was critical or whatever it was]. That was wrong of me. I am so sorry. Will you please forgive me?"

Be honest and straightforward. Do not defend, explain, or excuse your actions in any way.

Take responsibility for your actions. No matter how much strain you were under at the time, you are responsible for your actions. If you were wrong, admit it. Do not just say you are sorry. Take the next step and ask for forgiveness.

Anticipate Your Prodigal's Response

You are taking a different approach that may catch your prodigal off guard. She may weep and thank you for your confession. He may take this opportunity to yell at you and tell you many other things you did that hurt. Or he may say, "Oh, it was no big deal."

If you tried to justify, deny, or minimize your behavior in years past, your prodigal has probably done the same thing. Your goal is not to make her respond a certain way. Simply speak the truth and share your heart. Let your prodigal respond any way she chooses. Do not be surprised if she has great difficulty accepting your confession. Often there has to be more than one conversation.

Your prodigal may need time to absorb the impact of your message and respond accordingly.

Anticipate Your Response

How do you normally respond in tense situations? Do you wither under stress? When someone criticizes you, does your brain turn to mush and your legs become jelly? Do you find it hard to think and act?

Craig had a very honest and painful conversation with his prodigal brother. During the conversation, Craig's brother accused him of things he had never done. Craig was being attacked, and after a few minutes of his brother's barrage, he started slumping down in his chair. When he noticed what was happening, Craig sat up, strengthened his voice and his message, and reentered the conversation to address the truth.

Some of us respond in the opposite way. When we feel attacked or out of control, we take charge. We talk loudly. We give orders. We demand compliance. We intimidate people so they will give in to us. If you are trying to tell your prodigal you sinned against him and then react in anger if he doesn't immediately respond as you wish, you only add another layer of pain.

Know yourself. Anticipate any inappropriate reactions and compensate for them. In this case, make your confession, ask for forgiveness, and shut your mouth.

Forgiving means you do not bring up the offense again to the one you are forgiving. When God forgives, He removes our transgressions from us "as far as the east is from the west" (Ps. 103:12). Satan wants to dredge up every past sin to keep us locked in guilt. God, however, never uses the past to make us feel guilty.

Some of us keep reminding the prodigals in our lives of things they did wrong. Our hope is that the shame will force them to make better decisions.

In Jesus' parable, the prodigal son's father did not bring up his son's sins. He never mentioned them. When you forgive your prodigal, follow that example. Don't bring them up again.

Often family members are on opposite ends of the spectrum in their responses to stress. Some wither and others intimidate. They operate this way in other relationships. Now they want to do the same thing with the prodigal. Both need to understand their normal reactions and make specific plans to respond more appropriately.

End the Conversation with Grace

Initiating a discussion with your prodigal does not immediately resolve long-standing problems. It is, however, a major step in the right direction. Do not expect or demand that he embrace every word you say. He probably will not comprehend every detail you share. This dialogue merely opens the door for future conversations to restore trust.

This conversation is incredibly important. No longer will the prodigal feel she is solely to blame for the rift between you. When you take responsibility for your actions, she can more easily take responsibility for hers.

Make sure you do not get into an argument about the

past. Do not focus on who said what to whom. If your prodigal wants to argue, try to diffuse the tension by saying something like, "I really don't know about that. I didn't bring this up to blame anybody. All I want to do is tell you I'm really sorry for what I did and ask you to forgive me."

Arguing is a family sport in too many homes. Do not let your home be such a playing field. You need to replace arguing with love and understanding if you want to see permanent improvements in your relationships.

MAYBE YOUR PRODIGAL
HAS ALREADY TAKEN THE INITIATIVE

I spoke with a prodigal who told me sadly, "I've tried to talk to Mom and Dad several times. I know they are really mad at me, but they just won't listen to my side of things."

Prodigals sometimes try to mend fences, but family members may not hear what they want to hear. Maybe she said others were as much at fault as she was. Perhaps she blamed you entirely. But if she tried to take the initiative in the past and you verbally attacked or ignored her, she may be reluctant to try again.

Jacob told me that he tried to talk to his mother about how she had hurt him. His father was an alcoholic, but his deepest hurts came from his mother. When she was furious with her husband, she took her rage out on her three sons.

Jacob is the middle of the three boys. When he was in his forties, he lived far away from his childhood home. God brought healing in his life through his church. His father was dead, but Jacob wanted to try mending the relationship with his mother. He talked to his pastor to be sure he was saying the right things in the right ways.

Jacob first wrote out exactly what he wanted to say. Then he phoned his mother and told her he wanted to talk. He shared with her that he wanted to discuss some things that had hindered their relationship. She grudgingly agreed to listen. He always gave in to her rage before and absorbed all the blame. This time he was determined to speak the truth.

Jacob began by recalling some of his memories. He spoke of the hurtful words his mother spoke to him and his brothers. Jacob told her how those experiences hurt him deeply. She tried to interrupt a few times as he spoke, but he told her, "Mother, please let me finish."

When he finished, he waited for her reaction. She told him, "Well, Jacob, I do not know what you're talking about. None of those things ever happened."

"None of them?" he asked incredulously.

"Not a one. I'm not sure what you've been reading or who you've been talking to, but you grew up in a wonderful, loving home. Nothing like those things ever took place. Never."

His mother's reaction killed the flickering hope for an honest, loving relationship. Jacob found the courage to be honest. Maybe he could have said things better, but that wasn't the point. He took the bold step toward reconciliation, but his mother pushed him back.

You may know that your prodigal reached out to you in the past. You, however, were not ready to listen. When you talk with your prodigal, bring that up. Apologize for your response. It may be true that your prodigal did not get the facts straight. She probably blamed you instead of confessing her own sins. You, however, must remember your prodigal was making her best effort. Overlook what she said, and look into her heart. Find enough love and forgiveness to take the next step yourself.

REASONS WE DON'T ASK FOR FORGIVENESS

As we have seen, confessing our sins to others, especially to those who have hurt us, requires great courage. It is easier to continue blaming prodigals and feel justified in our self-pity in the role of victim. So why do we fail to approach our prodigal and ask for forgiveness? We keep finding excuses, such as the following:

"If we don't talk about it, I'm sure the problem will just go away." Problems that originate in childhood are not likely to just disappear. Like an infected wound, they fester until they consume our thoughts and hearts. In the short term,

ignoring the problems seem like a good strategy, but it turns out to be terribly destructive in the long run.

"It's not all my fault." Many of us remember past events over and over in our minds. The memories haunt us. We admit we made some mistakes, but so did our prodigals. We do not want to shoulder all the blame. We see conflicts as "all or nothing" issues: either we take responsibility for all of the problems, or we do not want to take responsibility for any of them. In time, we choose the latter.

Rather than seeing problems as all or nothing, we can begin to evaluate our own behavior. We can accept responsibility for our mistakes. We do not have to take responsibility for others' behavior.

"I didn't mean to hurt anyone." Sometimes we say harsh things in a fit of rage. Other times conflicts arise because of a genuine misunderstanding. Maybe we do something to protect one person that makes the other person feel neglected and unloved. We did not mean to hurt anyone, so we excuse ourselves. Excuses short-circuit forgiveness and maintain distance in the relationship.

"Surely he's over it by now." We are taught that time heals all wounds. When I talk to prodigals, I find that is not true. Wounds often are as fresh as ever. The initial confrontation happened so long ago that we can hardly remember the details. Time is no substitute for openness, honesty, confession, and love.

"Surely he's forgotten." Other times we clearly remember what happened. It bothers us, yet our fear of addressing the problems creates a strong hope that our prodigals have developed selective amnesia and forgotten them. We surmise, "Since he hasn't brought it up in years, I guess he doesn't even remember it happened." That is wishful thinking on our part, and it does nothing to resolve the rift.

"I'll just do it again." Many of us are sorry for our rage, name-calling, and other behaviors we inflicted on our prodigal. We do not want to talk about them because we are sure we'll do the same things again. Old habits and old beliefs die hard, but that is no reason not to try. A more realistic approach is to confess immediately each time we sin. We need to ask our prodigals to pray for us as we trust God to change us.

"I'm angry at him, and I won't forgive until he apologizes to me first." My father served as a soldier in the Korean War. The war, as you know, was never won or lost. It ended in a stalemate, with a demilitarized zone separating North Korea and South Korea. Today, both sides remain in the same positions they held years ago. Both sides continue to point their guns at each other, ready to blast the other if they make a false step.

Many family relationships are similar. We live in an armed truce, prepared for the other side to either apologize or fight to the finish. In the meantime, we simply sit back and wait.

"I don't know how he'll respond." Some of us have tried talking in the past, and it did not go well. We are afraid to try again because we are sure there will be another war if we bring up the hurts of the past. Even if we shoulder the blame, we fear our prodigals will use it to accuse us even more.

"If I ask for forgiveness, I'll have to change." Our prodigals sinned. They hurt us deeply. We feel like victims, and we act that way. We wallow in our pain. We gossip to our friends to get their sympathy. We spend hours thinking about what we expect to be done to make up for all the wrongs committed against us. If we confess our part in our strained relationships, we have to give up our comfortable roles as victims. It is much more difficult to take responsibility to speak truth, give grace, and become trustworthy in a difficult relationship. Many of us conclude that it is a lot easier to just stay the way we are.

CONFESSION AND FORGIVENESS ARE UNILATERAL

There is an underlying belief behind our excuses. If we take the initiative in reconciling with our prodigals, we think that they must also confess and repent. That simply is not true.

God calls each of us to walk with Him, even if those around us don't. In the same way, He calls us to confess our sins to one another, even if others do not respond well at all.

The response of others never defines our success. Our obedience to God does that. Paul wrote, "We make it our aim, whether present or absent, to be well pleasing to Him" (2 Cor. 5:9). We have an audience of One, the Lord Himself. What God thinks of our efforts is far more important than what our prodigals think. Jesus calls us to radical discipleship, to follow Him when everyone is looking, as well as when no one is looking. We must follow Him when we are accompanied by others or when we are alone in our faith.

Jesus told His followers, "If anyone desires to come after Me, let him deny himself, and take up his cross, and follow Me. For whoever desires to save his life will lose it, but whoever loses his life for My sake will find it" (Matt. 16:24–25).

Some reading this chapter are thinking, *I just can't tell my prodigal that I was wrong. It's too painful.* Jesus understands our pain, but He instructs us to deny our selfish desires to remain comfortable. He wants us to take up our cross of obedience and follow Him in doing what is right. When we do, He promises that we will find true life. We need to confess our sins to those we have hurt and seek forgiveness.

Stop blaming and confess.

Stop justifying and be honest.

Stop hiding and take action.

None of us can be sure how our prodigals will respond, but we can be very sure how our Lord will respond. He will say, "Well done, good and faithful servant."

IF THE PRODIGAL SAYS, "NEVER!"

Do not expect instant reconciliation. Occasionally prodigals respond to their parents' confessions with immediate heart-felt confessions of their own. In most cases, prodigals need time to process these surprising new developments in the relationship.

After a few days or weeks, they might gladly accept the confession and begin the process of restoration. Other times prodigals' bitterness causes them not to budge an inch. Their attitude is, *You hurt me badly, and now you're going to pay! I'm never letting you off the hook!* If this happens to you, here are some things to remember.

Choose to Forgive

Instead of harboring bitterness at your prodigal for his or her hard-heartedness, choose to forgive any offense just as you are choosing to forgive other past hurts. Forgive as quickly as you can and as fully as you can. Do not allow this hurt to turn into resentment and bitterness.

Release Your Guilt

All you can do is all you can do. You cannot undo the past. If you are honest with God and your prodigal about the past, you can be free of guilt. Remember, there is no condemnation for those who are in Christ. Absorb His great love and forgiveness. Do not let guilt continue to destroy your life.

Remove Obstacles

Try to remove anything that might inhibit the process of reconciliation. If you have been gossiping, do not do it anymore. If you have been lying to protect yourself, stop it. If you have been dishonest or unkind in any way, repent and change your behavior.

Be Trustworthy

In most cases, deeply wounded prodigals are reluctant to forgive because they think it means they have to trust someone who has hurt them. Your prodigal may be waiting for you to prove your trustworthiness. She will test your sincerity to see if you really want to build a relationship on love and honesty.

Earning trust takes time and tenacity. Do not give up because your prodigal insists on seeing genuine change in your life before trusting you. You probably have the same reluctance to trust him until you see genuine change.

You, however, can take the initiative and show him it can be done.

Asking for forgiveness is an act of great faith. It requires preparation, anticipation, and courage. Talk to your pastor, and pray for God's wisdom as you take this bold step.

Do not measure your success by your prodigal's reaction. Know that your faithfulness and obedience are pleasing to God. You never know. You may build a bridge between yourself and your prodigal. That bridge of love may support the first steps he takes on his road home.

- -

TRUTH TO REMEMBER

Honest conversations without excuses can remove barriers in your relationship with your prodigal.

- -

Chapter 6

. . . — — . . .

PRINCIPLE THREE: EXTENDING UNCONDITIONAL LOVE

LET ME TELL YOU THE STORY of two fathers whose families attend the same church in Tennessee. Both had daughters in high school.

One day several years ago, Joe's daughter, a seventeen-year-old junior, walked into the living room, where he was reading the newspaper. She sat on the sofa across the room without saying a word, and he didn't notice her at first. When he looked up a few seconds later to see her there, he noticed she had been crying. Her eyes were red and swollen. He put down his paper and asked, "What's wrong, honey?"

She looked down at the floor. "Mom told me I have to tell you myself." She began to sob.

Joe got up and crossed the room. He sat next to her on the sofa and put his arm around his dear daughter and told her, "Oh, it can't be that bad. Tell me what's going on."

"But it is *that* bad!" she shot back. "Daddy, I'm pregnant!"

Joe became rigid, and tears welled up in his eyes. They were not tears of sorrow and compassion. His were tears of rage. After a long, tense moment, he stepped away from his daughter and growled, "How could you do this to me? You know how I've tried to raise you, and look what you've done!"

She was crying uncontrollably now, but he continued his tirade. "You listen to me. I don't want this baby, and I don't want you. Get your things together and leave right now! Don't ever set foot in this house again. Do you understand me?"

She nodded meekly.

As he stormed out the door, he added, "You have made me ashamed to be your father." His daughter left that afternoon.

Joe's friend Frank was the pastor of their church. Six months after Joe's daughter announced her pregnancy, Frank told the congregation that he wanted to speak on a personal subject for a minute. He swallowed hard and began, "I want to tell you about something before you hear it from anywhere else. I asked my daughter if I could tell you, and she said yes. My sixteen-year-old daughter, Marianne, is pregnant, and as you know, she's not married. She told me the other day, and her heart was broken. She said, 'Dad, I've messed up, and I'm so sorry. Will you please forgive me?' She expected me to get angry, but my heart was filled with love for my sweet daughter. I put my arms around her, and I told her, 'I love you so much. There's nothing in the world you could do to keep me from loving you.'

"She looked at me through her tears and asked, 'But Dad, what about your position in the church? What will people say . . . about you?'

"I told her clearly, 'Darling, I don't care if they fire me from the pastorate or if they ask me to resign. I'm going to stand by you, no matter what.' So I want you all to know today that my daughter is pregnant. She will have the baby. Whatever assistance she needs, my wife and I will gladly provide for her. I don't approve of what she did, but she is my daughter, and I love her."

Guess which daughter is walking with God today? Joe's daughter is lonely and bitter. She is in her fourth marriage. Her father still expresses anger over her pregnancy, is still ashamed of her. She feels far away from her father and far away from God as well.

Frank's daughter is a vibrant Christian who has a wonderful ministry to unwed mothers.

Love and bitterness are both incredibly powerful. One has the power to heal; the other has the power to kill.

The father of the prodigal in Luke 15 challenges us to respond with unconditional love. While it is not necessary to approve of our prodigals' behaviors, it is necessary that we affirm our love for them regardless of their actions.

WHY WE DON'T LOVE UNCONDITIONALLY

The behavior of prodigals often embarrasses family members. Sometimes after I talk about prodigals in churches, parents tell me I do not understand. They explain in a whisper that their child is addicted to drugs . . . or in prison . . . or sexually active with someone who is not their spouse . . . or whatever. Then they follow this revelation with the self-evident disclosure, "And I am so embarrassed."

Let me make this very clear: Just because your child is living in sin, you have no right to love him or her less. God does not expect you to approve of your prodigal's behavior. He does expect you to love the person anyway. Unconditional love means we love our children for who they are, not what they do.

As we noted earlier, when we have one child living in sin and another walking with God, many of us portray one all bad and one all good. We cannot see any of the positive things the sinning child is doing. We overlook the faults of the "good child." Black-and-white comparisons make us less aware of the truth about both of them. Our love becomes more and more conditional as we deride one and elevate the other. Gossip and comparison drive the prodigal further away from God and from the family.

Some parents defend themselves by saying they do not want it to look as if they approve of sinful actions. Everyone, however, who knows them is well aware that they disapprove of their prodigal's sinful behavior. Do not use that excuse to keep you from loving your child unconditionally.

Did God insist that you and I straighten up before He loved us?

Paul said clearly, "But God demonstrates His own love toward us, in that while we were still sinners, Christ died for us" (Rom. 5:8). "While we were still sinners." That's when Christ made the supreme sacrifice and showed the depth of His great love toward us! Do you think Jesus' loving actions meant that He approved of our sins? Of course not, but Jesus did not demand that we stop sinning before He loved us. If He had, we would be in terrible shape.

Think of the prodigal son's father. That fine Jewish man, probably a leader in his community and his synagogue, had a son who was living with prostitutes and wasting money. As if that were not bad enough, he received word that his son had lost everything and was now feeding hogs! What could be more embarrassing? But that father did not let anything—neither his embarrassment nor the whispers of his friends—cause him to love his son any less. The moment his son returned, he was eager to pour out his love. Love overwhelmed any embarrassment.

A second reason we may fail to love our prodigals is bitterness. We become angry with them for acting so foolishly. Our anger gradually turns to resentment. Resentment, in time, festers into bitterness. The writer to the Hebrews recognized the threat that bitterness poses to relationships:

> Pursue peace with all men, and holiness, without which no one will see the Lord: looking carefully lest anyone fall short of the grace of God; lest any root of bitterness springing up cause trouble, and by this many become defiled. (12:14–15)

When Debbie and I married, I had a small garden. As I weeded it the first year, many of the weeds broke off just above the ground. They looked like they were gone, but in a few days a new weed was growing strong from the roots. I learned that I had to dig out the roots of the weed to prevent it from growing back.

In the same way, dealing with surface emotions and trying to look calm for our friends does not solve the problem of bitterness. A root of bitterness troubles everyone it touches. You must remove them. We have to eradicate the whole root of bitterness if we are to live in love and peace.

Bitterness prevents any closure or healing of pain. It

leaves us desiring revenge instead of healing and compassion. We may not think of our angry behavior as revenge, but that is exactly what it is when we gossip about our prodigal. We express it when we withdraw from her, when we find subtle ways of hurting him by giving a better gift to the "good child," or when we feel joy when the prodigal experiences hardships. We call it *justice* when he gets what we think he deserves, but *revenge* is a more accurate term.

Quite frankly, our bitterness probably affects us much more than it does our prodigals. It wastes our precious time on negative, destructive thoughts when we could be thinking of ways to honor God and help people. It eats away at our hearts and consumes us. It creates feelings of self-righteousness.

Bitterness saps our spiritual vitality. It grieves the Holy Spirit when we harbor resentment instead of forgiving. It erodes our joy in the Lord every day. We may still attend church services, sing the hymns, and even be in leadership, but gradually we begin to doubt God. We wonder, *How could God love me if He allows my son to do something like that?* Or, *Is God really sovereign? Is He really good?* If we do not root out the bitterness in our lives, we can pray for years with our prayers seemingly going unheard. We initially are hopeful. Then we feel disappointed and eventually become discouraged.

Many Christians have great difficulty acknowledging

their anger toward their prodigals. They believe that "good Christians don't get angry." So they smile through their bitterness and claim, "I'm not really angry, just disappointed."

A lack of honesty, however, prevents them from opening their minds to God's truth and their hearts to His grace and power. They stay in a prison of bitterness: alone and hopeless.

A third reason we fail to love our prodigals is that we have developed a habit of living at arm's length from them. In the beginning, we tried to help them change. When that did not work, we became resigned to coolness and distance in the relationship. We avoided talking about the real hurts because they were too painful. Besides, discussions about those things only bring more anger and discouragement. It is easier just to back off.

Distance begins as an emotional cushion, but quickly becomes a powerful barrier. Soon it becomes the norm for the relationship. Before long, we cannot imagine what it would be like to relate any other way. We become convinced: "I'm right. He's wrong. No change."

Love, however, does not use "being right" as an excuse to avoid reaching out to others. Jesus reached out to prostitutes and tax collectors. The loving father reached out to the prodigal son.

Love shines brightest when sin is darkest.

"I LOVE YOU IF . . ."

The Bible describes three kinds of love:

1. eros (sexual love),
2. phileo (brotherly love), and
3. agape (unconditional love).

Brotherly love is the basis for our friendships. We become friends with people because we have something in common with them: fishing, quilting, football, gardening, politics, or some other interest. As Christians, Christ calls us to a higher form of love—agape love—the way God loves us.

Brotherly love may be conditional: "I love you if . . ." or "I love you when . . ." But agape love has no conditions: "I love you in spite of . . ."

Far too often, we love people only because they make us feel good or contribute to our welfare in some way. Many of us love our families based on a list of mental criteria. If our loved ones meet our requirements, we smile and compliment them. If they do not measure up, we scowl and walk away.

What are some of the criteria we expect to be met? Here are a few examples of messages that some parents communicate in their attitudes and expressions, if not in these exact words:

- I'll love you if you are nice to me.
- I love you when you make me look good in front of my friends.
- I love you when you come to church and walk with God.
- I'll love you if you will get a good job like your sister has.
- I'll love you if you take time to call me every Sunday afternoon.
- I'll love you if you'll pay me back what you owe me.
- I'll love you if you'll stop neglecting your children.
- I'll love you if you stop acting like a fool and do what I think is right.

Jesus directs us to a higher definition of love. He tells us, "But I say to you who hear: Love your enemies, do good to those who hate you, bless those who curse you, and pray for those who spitefully use you" (Luke 6:27–28).

This sounds like the testimony of many parents of prodigals, doesn't it? Some prodigals hate us and curse us. Some spitefully use us. Even so, Jesus instructs us to take loving action toward them: do good to them, bless them, and pray for them. He continues:

But if you love those who love you, what credit is that to you? For even sinners love those who love them. And if you do good to those who do good to you, what credit is that to you? For even sinners do the same. And if you lend to those from whom you hope to receive back, what credit is that to you? For even sinners lend to sinners to receive as much back. But love your enemies, do good, and lend, hoping for nothing in return; and your reward will be great, and you will be sons of the Most High. For He is kind to the unthankful and evil. Therefore be merciful, just as your Father also is merciful. (vv. 32–36)

Let me draw a few conclusions from this passage:

- Being kind to those who are kind to you is no big deal to God. Even the heathen do that.
- If we go beyond what is normal and extend genuine love to those who do not love us, we are acting more like God. He is thrilled when we attempt to be kind to unthankful and evil people!
- Real love is openhanded, "hoping for nothing in return." Our love for others is genuine when we cannot assume they will appreciate it, now or in the future.
- If we choose to love those who do not love us, we will receive a reward someday. The reward

may be the return of our loved ones. It may be a future reward in heaven for our courage to love the unlovable.

YOU CANNOT GIVE WHAT YOU DON'T POSSESS

God doesn't expect us to draw water from an empty well. We can't give something that we don't possess, so God has gone to great lengths to give us the resources we need in order to offer unconditional love to others. I want to look at three passages of Scripture that encourage me. I trust God will use them to encourage you too.

Accept Others, Just As You Have Been Accepted

In his letter to the Roman believers, Paul wrote, "Therefore receive one another, just as Christ also received us, to the glory of God" (15:7). Our ability to accept others, especially those whose behavior is unacceptable to us, is found in knowing that Christ accepted us. Paul wrote that we were helpless enemies of God before we trusted Christ. That is pretty unacceptable, is it not? Yet God reached out to us and graciously met us where we were.

I think of many people Jesus loved. They were prostitutes, tax collectors, children, rigid religious people, confused people, and anyone who wanted to know Him. Many of these people were unacceptable to others. Jesus, though, accepted them without condemnation. He saw past their exteriors and looked at their hearts. He saw needs. With love, He met them.

Forgive Others, Just As You Have Been Forgiven

Paul also reminds us that God's forgiveness of our sins is the basis for our ability to forgive. He wrote, "Let all bitterness, wrath, anger, clamor, and evil speaking be put away from you, with all malice. And be kind to one another, tender-hearted, forgiving one another, even as God in Christ forgave you" (Eph. 4:31–32).

If someone is unwilling to forgive an offense, this passage suggests that the person is deficient in his or her personal experience of forgiveness. To put it another way, to the degree that we experienced God's forgiveness, we will be able and willing to forgive those who hurt us. That includes our prodigals.

Love Others, Just As You Have Been Loved

The apostle John identified himself in his gospel as "the disciple whom Jesus loved" (John 21:7). Did that mean he was the only one Jesus loved? Of course not, but the love of Jesus was so convincing and overwhelming that it became the very basis of John's identity. "I'm the guy Jesus loves so much," he probably told people along the road as the disciples followed their Master. There is, in John's writings, a gentleness and a kindness that flowed from his personal experience of the love of Christ. He wrote, "In this is love, not that we loved God, but that He loved us and sent His Son to be the propitiation for our sins. Beloved, if God so loved us, we also ought to love one another" (1 John 4:10–11).

Propitiation is an important word in our understanding of God. It means "to avert wrath." We, because of our sins, deserved the full wrath of God. His holiness demanded it against our sinfulness. Jesus' death on the cross was the sponge that absorbed the wrath so we would not experience it.

Thanks to Jesus, in place of judgment, God showers us with love. In place of the fires of hell, we receive His gracious presence. That is the measure of the love of God. John applied that measure to human relationships. He wrote, "Beloved, if God so loved us, we also ought to love one another."

Since the death of Christ averted God's righteous wrath so He could show us love, surely we can learn to show kindness to those who fall short of our petty standards.

Do these passages create a longing in your heart? Do you want to show this kind of unconditional love, forgiveness, and acceptance to your prodigal, but you simply do not know how? We cannot give it until we first let God work deeply in our own hearts. Then, out of the abundance of our own experience, we can offer these treasures to others.

One time Jesus went to the temple for the Feast of Tabernacles. Each day of the eight-day feast was more important than the day before. By the last day, the emotions of the crowd of pilgrims had reached a crescendo. In the middle of the commotion, Jesus made an important announcement:

> On the last day, that great day of the feast, Jesus stood and cried out, saying, "If anyone thirsts, let him come to Me and drink. He who believes in Me, as the Scripture has said, out of his heart will flow rivers of living water." But this He spoke concerning the Spirit, whom those believing in Him would receive." (John 7:37–39)

We cannot fake agape love. We cannot produce it ourselves. It is, however, available to us in abundance if we recognize our thirst and go to Jesus. In our need, we drink deeply of His grace. We learn that He forgives us even if we have hard hearts or when we let Him down.

We experience His kindness when we are hurting. We discover the depth of His love when we realize how unlovable we are. As the Holy Spirit works these truths into our hearts, we find a deep, full well of love, forgiveness, and acceptance for our prodigals.

STEPS TO TAKE

I am sure you want to love your prodigal unconditionally or you would not be reading this book. You may struggle with bitterness. The behavior of your prodigal may be embarrassing your family. Love, however, covers a multitude of sins. It covers your sins and the sins of your prodigal.

Let me give you some specific steps to take to begin to show a deeper level of love.

1. Be Honest About Your Lack of Love

First, be honest with God. If the Holy Spirit convicts you about your attitudes, words, and actions, especially toward your prodigal, agree with Him. Maybe your sin is failing to love your prodigal with the unconditional love of Christ. Let God's Spirit shine His light on your heart and give you insight about the quality of your love for your son or daughter.

2. Experience God's Love, Forgiveness, and Acceptance

Do not rush out to act on the next few steps until you have spent plenty of time letting God's grace sink deep into your own heart. You may need to reread this chapter. It may be a good idea to pray through the passages we addressed. Ask God to open your heart to comprehend His love more deeply. Focus on your own experience of agape love before you try to express it to your prodigal.

3. Give Your Blessings

The Old Testament patriarchs gave their blessings to their children. Abraham gave the blessing to Isaac (Gen. 25). Jacob then schemed to take away Isaac's blessing from his brother, Esau (Gen. 27). Finally, Jacob blessed his sons (Gen. 49).

All parents can give a blessing to their children that will provide confidence, hope, and strength. Let me suggest several ways your family can give your prodigal blessings.

Affirming words. Stop nagging. Stop condemning. Stop withholding kindness. Paul wrote, "Let no corrupt word proceed out of your mouth, but what is good for necessary edification, that it may impart grace to the hearers" (Eph. 4:29). Here's my translation of Paul's words: Shut up if you can't say something positive. Be sure to say things that encourage.

Our words come more from our heads than from our mouths. In other words, what we think about influences what we say. Analyze your thoughts to determine whether they honor God and edify the person who hears them. If they meet that standard, keep on thinking them. If not, replace them with positive thoughts.

Many of us think we have no control over our minds. That simply is not true. We are stewards of our minds just as much as we are of our wallets and schedules. You cannot expect to speak words of grace if all your thoughts condemn a person. The battle is fought primarily in our thought life. Fight hard, trust God, and win the battle.

Look for things your prodigal does well. You may have to look hard to find something positive to say. Learn again how to find actions you can affirm. If you practice diligently and trust God for wisdom, they will come.

Jake was on his deathbed. He wanted to speak some final words to a nephew and a niece. Both were prodigals.

Their mother (his sister) and their father had died years before. When the two adults came to see him, he told them, "I love you so much. I'm really proud of you, and I know your mother would be very proud of you."

He praised his nephew for being an amazing businessman, for working hard to attain such great success.

He turned to his niece, who had taught in high school, and told her, "You are a wonderful teacher. Your students are so blessed to have you care for them and teach them. You have modeled fine character for them every day. I know they will remember you the rest of their lives."

After his words of genuine praise, the old man continued, "But there's one thing that breaks my heart. You aren't in church anymore. You both have accomplished so much, but you are missing out on something that means a lot to me—a growing relationship with our Lord. Before I die, I sure wish each of you would make a commitment to go back to church and walk with God."

The nephew fidgeted, looked away, and mumbled, "I'll think about it." But the man's niece looked at him and said, "I promise you, next Sunday I'll go back to church. I promise I'll walk with God the rest of my life."

Sure enough, that same week she was in church, where she recommitted her life to Christ. Now, years later, she is strong in her faith and teaches Sunday school. She looks back on that day when her uncle affirmed her as a person and, in the context of his love, asked her to commit herself to God. He did not try to persuade her with guilt. Because he opened the door with kindness, she listened and responded.

Be sure you don't go overboard when you start using affirming words. If you say too much too soon, it will sound phony. It is better to say a word or two sincerely than to back up the dump truck with too many half compliments. When you begin, expect nothing in return. Your prodigal may be caught off guard. He might get angry because you waited so long to say things he longed to hear years ago. He probably thought he would never hear your words and will feel uncomfortable when you do express yourself. So speak simply and sparingly at first. Always speak with complete honesty.

Meaningful touch. Psychologists confirm what we know instinctively: physical touch is one of the most powerful ways to communicate love to someone. A kind hug or a pat on the back can mean more than you know to one who considers himself an outcast. Some families are huggers, and some are not. In the families that hug a lot, not hugging a prodigal communicates that he is unwanted and unaccepted. So in your attempt to reconcile, you may need to ask for permission to hug him again. Do not despair if he refuses out of his deep hurt. Your attempt is the first step toward opening the door to meaningful interaction, including hugging again when the time is right.

In the case of families who never hug, touch is not an option. It is a necessity to show genuine affection to someone you love in order to fill in the holes left by a lifetime of neglect. If hugging seems to be too threatening for the person, try a pat on the hand or the back, or simply a handshake.

Third-party compliments. Have you ever noticed how children beam with delight and pride when their parents tell a friend about their accomplishments in their presence? My children do.

Third-party compliments are powerful when wanting to assure someone you are sincere in your appreciation. Tell a friend, neighbor, or family member what you admire about your prodigal. If he's standing there, fine; if not, maybe he will hear about it later. Either way, you are sowing seeds of kindness and confidence. Who knows when and where they will spring up and bloom?

Meaningful gifts. Some of us use gifts to manipulate wayward family members. We gave in order to get something, or we withheld our gifts to make a point. Some of us passed along to our prodigals articles or messages on topics such as "How to Turn Your Life Around," "Why Stupid Decisions Are Destroying Your Life," or "Start Making Better Choices." If you're guilty of such "giving," stop. Instead, think about what the person values and give a present that says, "I understand what's important to you, and I love you." Consider giving a present to your prodigal when it's not a birthday or holiday. The gift does not have to be expensive at all, just something thoughtful.

Quality time. Some family members manage to spend lots of time in the proximity of their prodigals. Perhaps you take care of the prodigal's children or help out in some other indirect way. Other family members avoid being around the prodigal. If you already spend time helping them, think about how you might use that time to interact more personally. For example, you might tell your prodigal some good news about a friend of his or hers. Do not be gossiping but affirming. If there is distance in your relationship, begin by writing letters. Later try some phone calls. As the comfort level rises for both of you, consider face-to-face visits. Make the first personal visit very brief and positive. As your relationship strengthens, you can begin to spend more time together.

4. Take the Risk of Loving

The kind of love Jesus calls us to do is risky. He instructs us to give sacrificially. We are to expect nothing in return. If we harbor hopes that our prodigals will change magically and make us happy, we will probably be disappointed. Genuine love always involves risks:

- the risk that we will not be appreciated,
- the risk that we will receive anger in return for kindness, or
- the risk that as we move toward our prodigals, they will move further away.

We also take the risk that others will criticize us if we display unconditional love toward a prodigal. Their scorn quickly spreads to anyone who supports him or her. We need to remember that Jesus took a lot of criticism from the Pharisees for showing kindness to sinners.

If you show love to your prodigal, you may catch flak from the "Pharisees" in your church too. But that was the very reason Jesus told the parable of the prodigal son. He wanted to show the rigid, self-righteous religious contingent that God's heart was big enough to forgive even sinners.

The risk of loving is always a risk worth taking. Jesus took that risk with every person on the planet. Some accept His offer of love. Others reject Him.

Some keep Him at arm's length and others embrace His grace. Yet no matter how we respond, He keeps reaching out to show His love. He is the example we should follow in our relationships with those to whom we desperately want to communicate love and peace.

WATCH FOR SIBLING JEALOUSY

The bitterest person in some families is the prodigal's sibling. We all want attention, but when the attention goes to the one who is ruining his own life, resentment can occur. The faithful sibling often thinks, *I'm good to my parents. I go to church, and I pay my bills. I haven't been arrested, so nobody had to sit through my trial. I'm a responsible person, but my brother is a bum! Yet look at all they do for him!*

The "good kid" longs for family members to spend as much time thinking about her, talking about her, and praying for her as they do for her "no-good brother." She resents the prodigal for soaking up so much of the focused attention she wants to receive.

In addition, the wayward sibling may be squandering the "good kid's" inheritance. The prodigal may have stolen money from their parents. Family members often shell out thousands of dollars in bail money. Family members often give loans to the prodigal. The good kid knows she will not receive a dime from the prodigal. The good kid knows much of that wealth probably would have been hers one day.

The responsible child also feels she is not being rewarded for doing the right thing. She feels she deserves her parents' blessings for being responsible. She certainly does not feel she should be overlooked. Family members reward the prodigal with time and money while she, the responsible one, is left out in the cold.

If the good kid is jealous when her parents bail out her prodigal sibling, she may become furious when the prodigal comes home and the parents forgive him.

In Jesus' parable, the prodigal son's brother was jealous when he heard the celebration of his brother's return. He griped to his father, "It isn't fair!" That's the same sentiment many siblings of prodigals feel.

Watch for potential problems with sibling jealousy. Do all you can to speak the truth. You might need to apologize for times you preferred the prodigal over responsible family members. Show plenty of love to the ones who are faithful. Do not give them a reason to be jealous.

Parents also should write a clear will that outlines their intentions for how they want their estate to be divided. Do not assume your children will figure things out on their own and get along just fine. If one of them has been a prodigal, they probably will not.

LOVE OTHER PARENTS OF PRODIGALS

Perhaps the only people in your church who know what you are going through are other parents of prodigals. They experience the same pains and challenges. We need to be their most committed supporters!

I recently talked to a woman whose son is an alcoholic and a pathological liar. Years ago he married a woman whose mother was a good friend of his mom's. These two women had been friends since childhood. They took to being in-laws with great enthusiasm.

To no one's surprise, the marriage failed. The son lost all the money he made and ruined his reputation. The daughter had multiple affairs. Yet instead of comforting one another, the two mothers blamed each other's child for the failed relationship.

It has been fifteen years since the divorce. The mothers still live in the same small town and go to the same church, yet they have refused to speak to each other in all this time.

Every parent and family member of a prodigal can come up with plenty of reasons to feel angry. We need, however, to move beyond those things and focus on sources of healing. We need it for ourselves and for our children who are desperate for our unconditional acceptance.

Loving our prodigals unconditionally doesn't mean we must continually remove their pain. Unconditional love means loving our prodigals enough to practice tough love.

Encourage other parents when they are making the tough decision to let their prodigals face the consequences of their decisions.

- -

TRUTH TO REMEMBER

The greatest need your prodigal has is love without conditions.

- -

Chapter 7

· · · — — · · ·

PRINCIPLE FOUR: ALLOWING THE PAIN OF WRONG DECISIONS

A MOTHER IN HER SEVENTIES has a fifty-year-old son and two younger daughters. The son, Rick, is very bright . . . that is, except when it comes to work, women, money, and booze. Rick's father died when he was a boy. The family struggled financially. His mother worked hard to provide a decent life for her three children.

As the children grew up, everyone recognized that Rick was a gifted young man. Anger and insecurity, however, filled his heart. He began to drink when he was in high school. Police arrested him for driving while intoxicated, but he told his mother he'd only had a couple of beers. She believed him, blaming the policeman for being so harsh for such a small offense, and then paid his fine.

Following his graduation from college, Rick married his

sweetheart and found a good job. Then there were more arrests. Every time his mother paid his fine. Neither his job nor his marriage proved exciting enough for him. He soon quit both. His mother believed the problems were Rick's employer and his wife. Why? Rick told her they were the problem.

Rick wanted to start a new business, but none of his friends would become partners with him. Finally, he became desperate. He asked his mother for a loan. He promised to repay her within a year . . . eighteen months at the most. After seven months, the business folded. Neither Rick nor his mother mentioned the loan for a long time.

Rick took jobs with new companies in the budding field of technology, but he disliked working for somebody else. One year later he found someone who loaned him money for another new venture. This venture capitalist, though, was unwilling to put up all the money. Rick still needed about $15,000 more.

He called his mother and told her about this new deal. He explained that he would be able to pay her back the $15,000 plus the money he'd lost on the first business deal. She was skeptical. This time she consulted her attorney, who suggested a binding legal agreement. The mother, however, did not want to upset her son with demanding language, so she instructed the attorney to prepare a watered-down version. A few months later, his new venture went bankrupt, and all his mother had was a worthless piece of paper and his "good intentions."

Rick's drinking problem grew worse along with his financial problems. He was arrested again for driving while intoxicated and this time went to jail for it. Rick called his mother and told her, "If I don't post bail, they say they'll keep me for a week!"

His mother simply could not let that happen. She drove down to the police station and bailed him out. Outside the jail, she demanded, "Son, I'm sick of this! You'd better never let this happen again!"

Rick meekly replied, "You're right, Mom. This is the last time." She drove away in furious silence.

As a result of his latest arrest, the state revoked his license. He got another job but had no way to get there. His solution? He called his mother. She came and took him to work every day. She was angry, but she knew he needed to work if he was ever going to be able to pay her back. When he could not stand the shame of being like a preschooler with his mom dropping him off at work, Rick started driving again.

Rick's love life was not any better than his business life. Within a year, he got married and divorced two more times. His ex-wives took furniture his mother gave him. They were treasured pieces that she hoped he would value. But for each marriage disaster he had plenty of excuses. His wives were too bossy. They also expected to live the high life, which he could not provide for them. His mothers-in-law were too demanding, and they bad-mouthed him behind his back. His mother took his side each time and defended him to family friends.

One day two IRS agents visited Rick at work and ordered him to appear before a judge three days later. It turned out that he had failed to respond to their letters over the last two years. He owed twenty-two thousand dollars in back taxes, penalties, and interest. For that, the agents arrested him.

Rick called his mother and told her that he was in big trouble now. He might have to go to jail for three years if he could not come up with the money. His mother exploded, "Do you expect me to just give you twenty-two thousand dollars? After all the money I've given you, you haven't paid back a dime!"

Rick protested, "That's not true, Mom. I paid you back a thousand last year when—"

"A thousand dollars!" she interrupted. "You owe me almost a hundred thousand dollars, and you think paying me back a thousand dollars is really something?"

"Mom, this time I really mean it. If you'll loan me this money, I'll pay you back within a year. I swear, Mom," he pleaded. "I swear. Please, Mom. I don't want to go to prison."

She thought about her dear son going to prison for

three years. She could not bear the thought. She called her two daughters to get their opinions. Sarah was sympathetic: "Mom, I saw the movie *The Shawshank Redemption*. We can't let Rick go to prison! Horrible things happen there."

Suzanne, however, was more perceptive. She asked her mother, "And what will it be next time? How much will he ask you for then? Mom, you need to put a stop to it now."

Suzanne's attitude shocked her mother. She protested, "So you think it's a good idea for him to spend years in prison? After he gets out, he'll be a convicted felon. What kind of job can he get then? How will he pay me back if he can't get a job? Did you think of that?"

Suzanne stood firm. "If you keep bailing him out, he'll never learn his lesson. He'll just keep coming back for more. Look at his life since he graduated from college. It's been almost thirty years of nonstop trouble, and you have bailed him out every single time. He has made promises each time, and you've believed his lies. There's no end to it unless you stop bailing him out."

Rick's mom spent a long, sleepless night thinking about the massive amount of money she had loaned him in the past. She remembered the string of broken of promises, but then she thought of Rick's desperate situation and decided to ignore what she felt was Suzanne's hard heart.

At nine the next morning, she called Rick and told him she would have to get a second mortgage on her house because all her savings were gone. She brought a check to him. Rick expressed his deep gratitude, promising again that he would pay her back every cent.

It's been nine years since that incident. Rick is still drinking and driving. He just went through another marriage and divorce. After all the threats and promises, anger and guilt, nothing has changed. Nothing at all.

TWO INGREDIENTS

Good relationships, either among family or friends, require a blend of two vital ingredients: closeness and independence. We must learn to love other people, but without controlling them. Some call this "open-handed love" or "non-possessive warmth." We care for people, but we let them make their own decisions. If this delicate blend gets out of balance, we gravitate toward one of two extremes: isolation or enmeshment.

In some cases, fear or anger drives us away from others. It is easier to be alone than to risk closeness. In other situations, that same fear and anger creates insecurity in our relationships, so we try to control others any way we can. We convince ourselves that our nagging and demands are for their own good. We spend much of our time fixing people's problems and anticipating their needs. And prodigals certainly have lots of problems and needs, which consume us.

We come to believe that our willingness to help our prodigals validates our worth as family members. When we "fix" them, we feel strong. If we fail, we feel worthless and guilty. So our motto becomes:

If my prodigal has a need, I'll meet it.
If he has a little need, I'll make it into a big need.
Then I'll meet it.
If he does not have a need, I will create one.

REASONS WE FIX THEM

Prodigals, especially the embarrassing and defiant ones, mess up their lives in incredible ways. They have financial calamities, trouble with the law, drinking and drug difficulties, and neglected children. They marry people we dislike. They make decisions that are foolish at best. We see all this very clearly. Yet we feel the need to jump in to make it right.

Why are many family members of prodigals, especially parents, wired to fix the problems of their prodigals? Here are some reasons:

Their Failure Makes Us Look Bad

Arrest records, drug addiction, job loss, or unwanted pregnancies shame us. We, therefore, see our prodigals as a reflection of our family. If they look good, we look good. If they look bad, we look bad.

Every week we hear updates on other people's children:

- Ralph's son is now dean of men at the university ("the youngest man ever to hold that position," Ralph beams).
- Jenny's daughter has led thousands to Christ as a missionary in Lower Slobovia.
- Jerry and Wilma's grandson completed medical school.

We're glad for them, we say. Honestly, though, we are not that glad. We yearn to say something positive about our children or grandchildren. At least something better than, "Yes, we're really excited. Johnny's sentence was reduced from ten years to five. Isn't God wonderful?"

We Hope They'll Love Us for Helping Them

Let's face it: we all need love. We desperately want the members of our family to show us love and appreciation. So when they get in trouble, we think, *If I help him this once, surely he'll appreciate it. Surely he'll thank me. Surely he'll feel closer to me.*

We perceive our help as a type of bargaining. We give something and hope for something in return. We give money or time, and we hope our prodigals will love us for it.

I talk to many family members with prodigals who look

confused when they tell me about all the ways they have helped their prodigals and then conclude, "But no matter what I do, she doesn't appreciate it. In fact, we seem further apart now than when I started helping her."

They Demand Our Help

Prodigals become masters of manipulation. They whine that if we love them we will do whatever they ask. They often have a "victim mentality." Then they demand that other people fix their problems. "It's not my fault!" they protest. Loads of guilt fall on us when we do anything that they perceive as unloving. These prodigals, however, fail to look in the mirror and see that they are now adults who are responsible for their own decisions.

We Are Motivated by Tremendous Guilt

Parents mess up sometimes. No doubt about it. We fail our children in numerous ways. Then we feel awful about it. When our prodigals demand that we fix their problems, it triggers our compulsion to compensate for our shortcomings by doing whatever it takes to make them happy.

We become like puppets on a string: they pull and we dance. Guilt clouds our sense of self-esteem and security. It drives us to make decisions we would never make otherwise.

Many parents who are normally good money managers

give thousands of dollars to their irresponsible children be-cause they feel terrible about the past. Maybe these parents do so in order to compensate for their own failings—such as alcoholism, frequent rage, or a divorce. In most cases, they cannot pinpoint clear causes for the problems. They sim-ply surmise, "Since my child is having all these problems, it must be my fault."

Fixing Is a Hindrance

Every adult, including your prodigal, is responsible for his or her own behavior. Every adult is accountable to God and to family and friends for his or her decisions. When family members jump in to fix a prodigal's problems, they block God's redemptive work in that person's life. They hinder God from doing what He wants to do to bring change and redemption in that prodigal's heart.

Think back once more to the prodigal son after the "mighty famine" hit and he took a job slopping hogs. Jesus said that he longed to eat the pods the pigs were eating. It was then, and only then, that "he came to himself."

Repentance follows brokenness in the life of a prodigal. It never occurs before a broken spirit. What do you think would have been the outcome if his father had sent him sandwiches and soup every day? What if his dad had wired him some cash "just this once" to help him get through the hard time?

His father practiced tough love. He allowed him to continue trying to make it on his own. He allowed him to face the results of bad decisions. Then the wayward son realized his deep needs and gained spiritual perspective.

This is a crucial lesson for the family members of prodigals. We simply must follow the example of the father in Jesus' parable and let our prodigals experience the consequences of their decisions. If we step in and fix them, we short-circuit God's redemptive work. We find ourselves opposing God instead of working in tandem with Him.

As loving parents, we hate to see our children suffer. We want them to be whole, happy, and healthy. We, however, are blind. Guilt or pride prevents us from seeing the truth. We keep fixing our prodigals over and over again. We shield them from the stark realities of life. We prevent them from being angry with us. By removing the consequences of their actions, we also prevent them from growing.

THREATS AND OTHER LIES

"This is the last time I'm going to bail you out! Do you understand me? The last time!"

How many times have you said something similar to your prodigal? So many family members use threats, but they seldom follow through and allow their prodigals to experience the consequences.

Of course, our prodigals threaten us too: They threaten

to never speak to us again if we do not come through for them. They may even threaten to kill themselves. Whatever the situation, they always insist, "This is the last time." But then, so do we. We are both aware of the countering lies.

We train each other to disregard our words because actions are what really matter. One prodigal told me, "When I'm in trouble, my mother yells at me and fusses at me, but in the end she always comes through." Underneath all the threats and promises, both parent and prodigal know that no amount of yelling, blaming, arguing, sulking, or crying will change things. Too many parents are simply unwilling to make the hard decision to quit bailing out their wayward kids.

In the place of truth, parents offer excuses for why their children keep ruining their lives. They say:

- "She can't help it. She's always been that way."
- "It's not his fault he got fired. His boss is a real jerk— just like the last one."
- "Oh, divorce isn't all that bad. The grandkids will probably be better off anyway."
- "I'm sure it won't happen again. Look at all the trouble it caused. Surely he'll learn from this mistake."

These, too, are forms of lies. Such excuses attempt to minimize the damage and excuse the foolish person from taking responsibility for destructive decisions. Facing reality is incredibly difficult for our prodigals. It is also difficult for the parents. We are lying to ourselves if we think we are genuinely helping them by fixing their problems.

Dr. James Dobson wrote a best-selling book entitled *Love Must Be Tough*, in which he addresses this very point. Fixing prodigals does not help them at all. In the long run, it hurts them. Threats sound tough. They allow us to bluster and sound authoritative, but if we do not follow through with what we say we are going to do, our words are worthless. In fact, we lose ground because our children learn that they cannot trust our words.

HOW DOES FIXING HURT THE PRODIGAL?

Attempting to fix all of our children's problems can be more devastating for them than we realize. It may bring temporary relief, but in the long run it prevents them from learning valuable lessons that can change their lives. Consider the following potential results when parents get too involved too often.

Fixing Creates False Expectations

I talk to men and women as old as sixty who tell me, "It doesn't matter how much I mess up. My family will always find a way to fix things."

These supposedly adult children have the psychological

development of preschoolers. They learned to be helpless because they know someone else will make everything right. All they need to do is whine, and the "Lone Fixer" will ride in and solve their problems. They have developed false and dangerous expectations.

Fixing Prevents Justice

Prodigals whose problems are solved by their parents have a warped view of justice. They fail to realize that people reap what they sow. Their parents usually bypassed that important principle in their lives. Whenever they have a problem, they automatically seek an easy bailout. Ironically, when other people face difficulties, these same prodigals are often quick to condemn them for their foolishness.

Fixing Teaches Them to Be Irresponsible

Pampered prodigals fail to learn the hard lessons of responsibility. They think that it is too much trouble to do what is right. Besides, it's not much fun anyway. They live for the pleasure of the moment. They never learn to value time, money, people, or commitments. Becoming responsible requires wisdom and endurance. If family members bail out prodigals every time they have problems, they prevent them from emotionally growing up. Rescuing prodigals reinforces the belief in the mind of a prodigal that there is no need to keep commitments they make.

Fixing Prevents Brokenness

God loves "a contrite heart" (Psalm 51:17). Many of the psalms and other passages of Scripture tell us that God delights in people who humbly admit that they are needy. Jesus said, "Blessed are the poor in spirit, for theirs is the kingdom of heaven" (Matt. 5:3). When you bail prodigals out time and time again, you develop calluses in their hearts. Each instance adds another layer, which makes it even more difficult for prodigals to soften their hearts.

But nothing is too difficult for God. He wants your prodigal to "come home" even more than you do. I know that God orchestrates many of the difficulties our prodigals face, but when we step in, we interfere with His work and preempt the messages He wants them to hear.

Fixing Perpetuates Manipulation

Lies and manipulation become a cycle between parents and prodigals when parents threaten not to bail their kids out but do so anyway. In return, prodigals promise to change but never do. It is like a dance that never ends. It becomes an ugly dance of controlling behavior, guilt, and ruined hopes.

By now you may be thinking, *But what about unconditional love? In the last chapter you told me to love unconditionally, but now you are telling me to stop helping. If I do that, she'll believe I don't love her. I'm confused.*

Unconditional love is much more than simply making

someone happy for a while. It is doing whatever it takes for that person's ultimate well-being. Unconditional love often affirms, but sometimes it must cut like a surgeon's scalpel in order to remove the tumor of sin. Sometimes a doctor must cause a little pain to effect long-term healing. In the same way, love dictates that we speak the truth and require real change. Anything less is not love. It is only sentimentality, which is a poor substitute for the real thing.

THE COURAGE TO STOP FIXING

I love *The Andy Griffith Show*. Andy was a paragon of virtue. Barney Fife, his deputy, was . . . well, Barney. In one episode, Andy's son, Opie, had a conniving friend, Arnold, who told him, "I know a way you can get anything you want from your dad."

"How can I do that?" Opie asked him.

"If you ask him and if he says no, just hold your breath 'til you turn blue. He'll panic and give you anything then!"

"Wow!" exclaimed Opie. "I gotta try that!"

Opie went to the sheriff's office to see his father, and he told him, "Pa, I want you to triple my allowance."

"Well," Andy began slowly, "I don't know about that, Opie. Naw, I just can't do that, son."

Opie insisted, "But I really want it, Pa!"

Andy was not going to give in. "No, Opie. I said you can't have it."

Opie took a deep breath and held it. Andy watched as Opie's face turned red. Finally, Opie could hold it no longer. He gasped for a breath. He looked confused. Finally, Andy asked him, "Opie, what in the world are you doing?"

Opie answered, "Holding my breath 'til you give me what I want."

"At least it's good for your lungs," Andy told him as he walked off.

Opie told Arnold that his trick did not work. Arnold, though, was going to do whatever he wanted to do. Barney repeatedly told him not to ride his bike in the street. Arnold kept ignoring him.

Finally, Barney told him to stay out of the street "or I'll impound your bike, young man. I sure will!" The boy did not believe Barney's threat, and moments later he almost ran over Sheriff Taylor! Barney, ever the watchful deputy, saw the whole scene and made good on his promise. He grabbed Arnold and impounded his bike.

In the sheriff's office, Andy told the boy to bring his father in for a talk. Soon the father swaggered into the station and demanded, "Sheriff, you can give me the bike now."

Andy replied in his wise way, "It's not quite that simple. Your son needs to stay off the street, or I'm going to keep that bike until he learns his lesson. If he rides in the street one more time, I'll have to put you in jail."

The boy pounded the sheriff's desk angrily and yelled

at Andy, "You can put my daddy in jail, just give me my bike!"

The boy's selfishness surprised his father. He turned to Andy and told him solemnly, "That's okay, Sheriff. Give me the bike. I'm going to sell it."

Hearing his father's words, the son pitched a fit. Andy watched the tirade, then told the father, "Sir, in case you're wondering, there's an old-fashioned woodshed out back."

His father immediately led Arnold out back to have the *board of education* applied to the *seat of learning*. Like the father in this episode, some of us need to step back, take a good look at our prodigal's attitude and actions, and change *our* behavior.

Righting wrongs requires courage. No matter what it takes, we must become partners with God instead of road-blocks to His work. The courage to stop fixing our prodigals requires three things: perspective, a plan, and support.

Perspective

A father told me his son lost his job again. He always had problems holding a good job. He always blamed his boss, the company, vindictive coworkers, or something else for his failures. His father believed his story every time and made calls to his friends to try to find his son a new job.

Time after time, his friends pointed out, "His résumé and references aren't all that good."

But the dad pleaded and promised, "This time will be different."

His friends would reluctantly hire the young man, but after a few months the same patterns would emerge, and he would again be fired. This loving father finally told his son, "I want you to look at what has happened in the last five places you've worked." His son started to defend himself, but the dad continued, "Son, both of us have to face the facts. You have lost these jobs because you have acted irresponsibly."

Again, the son tried to jump to his own defense, but again the father silenced him. "And son, this has got to stop. First, I want you to know I'm not going to ask any of my friends for a job for you. That's final. You are going to have to find one on your own. I'm not going to support you while you are looking for a job. And I'm not going to lie to my friends about your problem. I won't say anything unless they want to know, but if they ask, I'm going to tell them you are learning some valuable lessons about responding to authority. I will be glad to advise you, but I'm not going to get involved directly anymore. What I have done up till now hasn't helped, as much as I wanted it to. In fact, I really think all my efforts have hurt you by keeping you from being realistic about your behavior."

During this carefully planned statement, the son fumed. At his first opportunity he exploded in a tirade of accusations.

"If Mother were here, she wouldn't let you get away with treating me like this! She loved me!" Then he growled, "I wish you had died instead of her!"

The father remained calm. "Sometimes I wish the same thing, son. But I'm here, and she's not. And actually, I've thought a lot about what your mother would want, and I'm convinced she would agree that if I really loved you, I'd insist on more responsibility from you."

This father did a magnificent job of confronting reality and speaking with clarity. He did not yell. He did not curse. He simply spoke the truth and explained what he was doing. All that was left was to follow through with what he had said.

When we see that threats and broken promises aren't working, change is absolutely mandatory. If we continue to believe lies and fix problems, we perpetuate irresponsibility.

We need a new perspective, one that shows us we cannot control our prodigals' behavior. We can speak truth, and we can pray. We need to, however, let our prodigals make their own decisions. We need to muster the courage to open our hands and let go if they decide to turn their backs on us. We can only control our choices, not theirs. They are free to come or go. They can act responsibly or irresponsibly. It is the best opportunity for allowing them to reach a point of repentance.

A Plan

Anytime we chart a new course in our lives, we need a plan. If you want to take up quilting, you learn from others. You design your pattern and find the fabric you will need for the job. If you want to learn to fly-fish, you watch people who have perfected the art of dropping a dry fly at the head of a pool so it can drift past a submerged rock where a trout is waiting for its next bite. We need a plan when we travel, plant a garden, bake a cake, or install software on our computers. We also need a plan when we want to make changes in the crucial relationships with our prodigals.

I suggest you write out your plan carefully, with the input of someone who has successfully dealt with the same problem. Keep in mind that success is not determined by the prodigal's response but by the parents acting in a responsible way to avoid fixing the prodigal's problems any longer. Your plan needs to focus on addressing the patterns in your prodigal and in yourself. They will be painfully obvious, but do not shy away from writing them clearly and boldly. Stay focused on the big things: irresponsible behavior, promises and threats, and meaningless gestures. Also list the excuses that prevented you from seeing the truth.

In your plan, take responsibility for your own behavior. If you believe lies, determine to quit. If you have been blocking God's work by fixing problems, admit as much.

A friend of mine who had been rescuing his sister for years began his talk with her by saying, "I want to apologize for the way I've treated you." She looked surprised. He continued, "I have bailed you out again and again. I hoped it would make you love me more, and I hoped it would make me feel good about myself. That was selfish of me, and sinful. Please forgive me." He then explained that he would no longer fix her problems.

Your plan needs to include a "next time" clause. Make it clear what you will do the next time your prodigal needs help. Some of us are so well-trained that we jump to help before we are even asked. Learn to say the word that all fixers must learn: "No."

Shortly after you tell your prodigal you are not going to fix him any longer, you can be sure he will test you. Sooner or later, he will have a crisis and then expect you to come to his rescue. Take a deep breath and say, "I'm sorry you're in trouble again, but like I told you, I'm not going to solve your problems any longer. I love you, and I want the very best for you. The best for you in this case is to experience the consequences of your choices."

Your plan also should anticipate your child's reaction and prepare you for it. Be strong. Do not cave in to accusations. No matter how guilty you feel, do not give in and rescue the person again. Stay in control. If you anticipate these reactions, you will not be caught off your guard.

Planning is a vital necessity in changing your relationship with your prodigal. Even if you are good at winging every other area of your life, this one is different. This relationship cuts to the core of who you are. It's like nothing else in your life, so be prepared. Plan well.

Support

Have you read the warnings on some toys, "Use only under adult supervision"? The same is true for changing how we relate to prodigals. We benefit greatly from the insight, encouragement, and support of a trusted friend, pastor, or counselor. Most of us fly solo so long that we are blind to reality. We have called lies "truth." As a result, we excuse sin. Now that we realize we need to change, the complexity and confusion of the relationship can overwhelm us. We are not sure how much slack to give, if any, to our whining prodigals. It is easier to go back to the old ways and rescue them "just one more time."

Choose your counselors wisely. Some people have simplistic solutions, like: "Just love him. Everything will turn out all right." Others like to avoid conflict in their own lives, so they advise you to do the same. A few will recommend drastic solutions, such as, "Kick him out and never let him see the door again! He deserves it!" Some spiritualize the relationship: "If you just pray, I am sure God will change your son's heart."

Perhaps you have received such advice before. Each suggestion has a smattering of insight that makes it deceiving. Find someone who understands the difficult issues of responsibility and love, and draw wisdom and strength from that person as you go through this process.

The person who gives you perspective may also help you clarify how you and your spouse differ over how to handle your prodigal. In most families, the mother and father have different solutions to the problem. One is passive, the other aggressive. One wants to avoid conflict; the other demands compliance.

Many of the heartaches family members of prodigals endure involve more than the prodigal. Disagreement with a spouse or other children over the proper course of action can cause confusion. Most people try to talk about their disagreements in the early stages of their prodigals' difficulties.

Frequently, though, they settle into patterns of quiet anguish or volcanic explosions that generate ongoing pain. Your pastor, counselor, or friend will notice how the strain of parenting a prodigal is affecting your marriage. You can seek healing in this relationship too.

YOU CAN EXPECT . . .

We touched on this topic earlier, but I now want to address it directly. When you stop fixing your prodigal's problems, you can expect her to fight you in every way she can. Her goal is to get you to back down and go back to the old way of rescuing her. She will do whatever it takes to make that happen.

You are familiar with her tactics, whether it's self-pity to melt your heart or vicious name-calling to coerce you into action. She may accuse you of not loving her "as much as you love" her brothers or sisters. She may threaten to hurt herself if you do not come through this time. If she used guilt in the past, she will try to make you feel guilty again. If she intimidated you in the past, she will do that again. Count on it. Be ready for it.

If you stay strong for a few days or a few weeks, do not think it is over.

Like a prizefighter who holds back and waits for just the right opportunity, your prodigal may strike the moment you drop your guard. Many parents weather the initial onslaught but eventually wilt under the pressure.

If you feel you are going to cave in, buy some time. Say, "I need to think about this for a day or two. I'll get back to you."

Then call your friend, counselor, or pastor to get the encouragement you need to stay strong. Whatever it takes, do not go back to the same destructive pattern that has been a dead end for so many years. Weather the storm. When you convince your prodigal you are steadfast, she will finally accept it. She will not like it, but she will realize you are not going to back down.

At that point, she has a choice. This could be her best chance to get out from under the bad habits that lead to her failures and to adjust her expectations and establish a new relationship with you based on honesty and respect. Perhaps she can look candidly at her own life, genuinely repent, and turn to God for healing and hope.

TEST YOUR CHILD'S SINCERITY

Hearing our prodigals say, "I'm sorry. I'll never do it again" thrills us. Family instinct drives us to let down our guard and trust them. We need, however, to be a bit more careful. Actions speak louder than words. We can be happy for the good intentions they express, but we must witness genuine change. No matter how our prodigals respond, we can offer forgiveness. Forgiveness can come in a moment, but trust will take time. Our beloved prodigals need to prove they are trustworthy.

Joseph was sold into slavery by his brothers, taken to Egypt, falsely accused of adultery, and thrown into prison. He languished there for years until God sent the pharaoh's baker and cupbearer to prison. Joseph interpreted their dreams. Later, when the pharaoh's dreams troubled him, the cupbearer told him about this remarkable young man. Joseph interpreted the pharaoh's dreams and became the second in command over all of Egypt.

Famine hit the land. Eventually Joseph's brothers, without realizing who he was, stood before him to buy grain. In numerous conversations, Joseph tested them repeatedly and specifically to see if they were the same as long ago. He even threw them in prison for three days. Then he ordered all but one to return to their father and bring back their youngest brother, Benjamin.

The brothers felt pangs of guilt and speculated that God was chastening them for betraying Joseph. Joseph heard their expressions of grief and guilt. Yet they had no idea he understood them. Still, he kept testing them. They passed a test of honesty involving a silver cup hidden in their grain. Then, at a feast, Joseph arranged for Benjamin to receive five times more food than any of the others to see if the older brothers would reveal any hidden jealousy. They passed all the tests. The brothers were different from the days when their envy caused them to sell Joseph.

As a final test, Joseph made it appear that Benjamin had committed an offense worthy of death. The brothers immediately begged to take Benjamin's place. Instead of betraying their brother, they were ready to sacrifice their lives for him.

Their actions satisfied Joseph. Repentance had brought change in their hearts. Joseph then revealed his identity. Reconciliation began.

Follow Joseph's example. Test your prodigal thoroughly. Institute tests to see if he or she is trustworthy. Do not make any premature assumptions. Be wise and be specific as you plan your tests.

Sadly, although some prodigals will prove to be trustworthy, many will not. Often family members make the mistake of trusting too much too soon.

Many of us resist testing others. Perhaps it does not seem like testing and forgiving can go hand in hand. Maybe we fear we will discover that our prodigals really do not want a relationship with us. Some of us believe that when we forgive, we must also trust the person. That simply is not true. Our Lord commands us to forgive because it frees us from bitterness.

We can institute tests, just as Joseph did, to determine the degree that people are worthy of our trust.

IS IT EVER APPROPRIATE
TO GET INVOLVED AGAIN?

Having said all these things, we also need to acknowledge there might be times when it is good for you to step in and help your prodigal again. Just be careful that you are acting appropriately.

Do not rescue your prodigal if his predicament is the result of sin or irresponsibility. If he has a car accident, for example, helping him is a loving response. (The situation gets a bit more awkward if the accident was the result of his drunk driving. In that case, you may want to offer physical assistance, but not financial help.)

If the prodigal is a son-in-law or daughter-in-law, try to relieve your child's suffering without bailing out the prodigal. In-law issues can be particularly difficult because any direct help you provide for your child is care the prodigal should be providing. The best way to help your child in such cases might be to obtain help from a pastor, counselor, or lawyer to help the child find meaning, purpose, sanity, and direction for the future.

Another time to step in is when there is neglect of your grandchildren. If they need food or clothing, take the items directly to their house. Do not give money to your son or daughter. Spend time with your grandchildren, yet try to avoid perpetuating your prodigal's irresponsibility. As much as possible, do not let your grandchildren suffer. Be there for them. Get advice from your friend, counselor, or pastor about your role in a delicate situation like this.

Significant change can be threatening. Think and pray diligently to get God's perspective. Learn what love really is. Understand love sometimes is tough. Let God produce genuine convictions in your heart that will equip you to get beyond the guilt you are likely to feel when you take a stand. Communicate your decision clearly. Stand strong in the face of opposition. You risk seeing your prodigal walk away, but you also provide the opportunity for genuine repentance and reconciliation. It's worth it.

- -

TRUTH TO REMEMBER

If family members help prodigals avoid the consequences of their actions, they will remain prodigals. Love requires you let your prodigal accept responsibility.

- -

Chapter 8

. . . — — . . .

PRINCIPLE FIVE: WATCHING YOUR WORDS

THE OLDER LADY looked at me as if I were a green alien from Mars. She was incredulous. She began to tell me about her son's explosive temper and all the pain it had caused. Moments later, I simply asked her, "What do you appreciate about your son, Mark?"

"Appreciate?" She shook her head. "Well, Phil, I'm not sure I can think of a single thing. Mark has messed up his own life, his family, and my life too. As far as I'm concerned, and I hate to say this about my own son, he's a first-class jerk."

I had a sneaking suspicion she did not hate saying it all that much. She continued telling me her son's story. Mark kept his temper under control most of the time. When it blew, it was like a volcanic eruption, devastating everything in its path. His wife, Beth, or their two children could say something they thought was innocent, but Mark would explode.

Beth tried to talk to his mother a time or two about the fear she and the kids felt around Mark. His mom told him, "Mark, I'm ashamed of you. You are ruining your marriage, and you're a terrible father. You'd better change your ways right now!" Of course, this "encouragement" did not make him more compliant. Instead, his rage became more intense.

To everyone else, Mark seemed to be the picture of Christian maturity. He sang in the choir and prayed fervently in prayer meetings. He went on the men's retreat and sang a solo that almost moved some of those crusty guys to tears.

Yet one day Mark walked in and told Beth he did not want to be married anymore. It stunned her. She pleaded with him to stay, but he refused. He moved out that day and rented a furnished apartment across town.

Beth went to his apartment that night to try to talk him into coming back home. A friend of Mark's named Martha opened the door. Beth was speechless. Martha stammered a weak explanation, but Beth knew. Mark came to the door and exploded at Beth. "How dare you come here! You have no business prying into my life!"

"Bu . . . but," Beth stammered as she protested, "but we're still married."

Mark shouted, "Not in my book, we're not!" and he slammed the door.

In a couple of months, a judge finalized the divorce. The next day Mark married the "friend." Seven months later, Martha gave birth to an eight-pound baby.

During the divorce proceedings, Mark's church tried to intervene on Beth's behalf. Mark came up with plenty of explanations. Fortunately, the pastor refused to overlook the fact that he was committing adultery. Mark left the church. Soon he and Martha joined one nearby. The pastor there was glad to have an accomplished addition to the choir. He was happy to give Mark and his bride a fresh start on a new life together. Mark starred in musicals, and Martha sang in the choir too. While Mark seemed to be doing just fine, Beth and her children struggled.

In reality, Mark was *not* doing fine. About a year after the birth of their child, Martha went to their pastor and told him horror stories of Mark's explosions at her and the baby. She lived in fear and did not know what to do. The pastor asked Mark to come for counseling. Mark arrived the next day with Martha. He was the picture of repentance and meekness. The pastor felt that God had worked a miracle. The next week Martha called the pastor again in the middle of the night to tell him she had called the police to protect herself and the baby from Mark's rage. The judge issued a restraining order to keep him away from them for a month.

It was at this point that Mark's mother was telling me his story. After she finished, I asked her the same question I had asked at the beginning, "I understand that your son has made some terrible mistakes. But what is one quality that you appreciate about him . . . one strength you see?"

She gave me that same blank look and began to speak as if I had a single-digit IQ. She said, "Phil, you just don't understand. My son is a jerk. Who but a real jerk would treat his wife—actually, both wives—his children, and me this way? There's nothing good to say about him. Nothing at all." Then she had a flash of insight: "If I don't tell him how messed up he is, who will?"

Some of us become so upset with our prodigals that their behavior consumes our thoughts. We can talk for hours about all the details of their faults. Yet we cannot think of one good to say about them.

Our tongue has great power. It can heal or it can destroy. James wrote:

> The tongue is a little member and boasts great things. See how great a forest a little fire kindles! And the tongue is a fire, a world of iniquity. The tongue is so set among our members that it defiles the whole body, and sets on fire the course of nature; and it is set on fire by hell. . . . But no man can tame the

tongue. It is an unruly evil, full of deadly poison. With it we bless our God and Father, and with it we curse men, who have been made in the similitude of God. Out of the same mouth proceed blessing and cursing. My brethren, these things ought not to be so. (James 3:5–6, 8–10)

Our thoughts influence our words. If our thoughts are negative, our words will be full of condemnation. If our thoughts are hopeful, we will find affirming words to say. The problem, of course, is that many of us have lost hope. We are so deeply hurt, and our prodigals have been in the far country so long, that we gave up long ago.

In order to think positively, we need God to refresh our hearts with His grace. God can and will use anything for good if we trust Him. If your prodigal disregards His blessings, perhaps the hard times will get his attention. God is at work whether we can see His plan or not. He is near whether we can sense His presence or not. Trusting that God is sovereign and good changes our mental outlook. Positive thoughts about God's character and His desire for us and our prodigals erode a negative, critical, harsh attitude.

MESSAGES WE SEND

Some of us are so angry that venom spills out of our lips. We do not try to be critical. It just comes naturally. Our thoughts and hearts reflect bitter hopelessness, so our mouths utter harsh statements. We say them a thousand times until they feel right. They reflect what we truly believe, but they are devastating to us and to our prodigals.

Here are a few statements I've heard parents say to their children:

- "You'll never make anything of your life."
- "I've tried so hard, but now I just can't stand you!"
- "You're not as sweet and loving as your sister."
- "I hate to say it, but I wish you'd never been born."
- "You're such a jerk!"
- "I don't even want to be seen with you."
- "You're such an embarrassment to me."
- "Why are you so stupid?"
- "I don't know what to think about you anymore."

Many of us recognize the destructive power of words like these, so we avoid using them. Instead, we are more subtle. I overheard a man talking to his son and a friend. His son had recently lost his job. It embarrassed his father. He tried to help his son get a new job, but nothing worked out. The friend was talking about his terrific job: a good salary, benefits, three weeks of vacation, and on and on. When the friend finished, the father looked at the ground and said, "Well, son, if you had played your cards right at your old job . . ."

The son had heard plenty of "ifs" and "buts" from his dad over time. He sighed. "I know, Dad. I know I've messed up my life. You don't have to keep reminding me." The father's words weren't terribly harsh, but they were like Chinese water torture: constant dripping that eventually wore his son down.

Quite often, criticizing others is a way of controlling them. If we put them down, maybe they will feel guilty enough to do what we want them to do. Criticism exalts us as it puts others down. We become masters at identifying everything that is "wrong" with others: their clothes, their hair, where they go on vacations, the way they talk, their hobbies, and their church attendance. Misery loves company. If we lack joy, we resent people who do. We criticize them in an attempt to bring them down to our level of despair.

Let me share some ways you can guard your thoughts and speak words of life instead of death, light instead of darkness.

CORRECT SPARINGLY

The main communication principle in almost all relationships is to correct sparingly and affirm specifically. Let us first focus on correction.

Do not nag your kids.

Do not tell them what they are doing wrong. They already know that!

Make a list of the messages you've said to your prodigal during the last month. Which ones were affirming? Which ones were critical of him and his behavior? In addition to any outright condemnations that come to mind, also consider ones that are underhanded and subtle.

There is a big difference between correction and criticism. The purpose of criticism is to control. We use it to hurt a person who hurts us. We use it to make her feel guilty so she will do what we think is right. Even as we accuse our prodigals of being manipulative, we try to manipulate them through criticism.

Correction, in contrast, is not self-focused. Its goal is real change. Its motive is hope. We must use correction sparingly and choose our words carefully so they will have power. Occasional correction can open hearts. Too much correction hardens them.

Do not nag your children about their church involvement or the lack of it. I know some family members who call prodigals on Sunday afternoon to say, "I noticed you weren't in church this morning." I know others who try to put the squeeze on their children by telling them, "We're having a special program next Sunday, and I promised the pastor you would be there. Don't let me down." Invite your children back to church, but do not pressure them. When they show up, do not make a big deal of it. Just say, "I'm glad to see you. I hope you enjoy the service."

My father told me a story about a prodigal young man whose mother attended the Brush Arbor Revival Meetings when my father was a boy. She seldom went to church, but she always "got right with God" during the revivals. As soon as they were over, however, her life returned to its normal state of apostasy. Her son showed up at the revival one night. The woman was happy. At the end of the meeting, she ran down the aisle and told him, "Come on, Son. I want you to go to heaven with me!" He calmly replied, "That's all right, Mom. I won't go tonight because you'll be going back again next year, I'm sure."

Also avoid making a habit of correcting or criticizing your child's spouse. If you plant seeds of discontent about your son-in-law or daughter-in-law, you could damage the relationship more than you realize. If your daughter complains to you about her husband, do not reply, "I told you he was no good. If you had listened to me, you'd have dumped that bum a long time ago!" You may feel very negative emotions about your child's spouse, but do not share them. At the right time and place, you may have the opportunity to express yourself honestly to attempt to correct a wrong that you see in their relationship. Even then, you must speak sparingly and wisely.

AFFIRM SPECIFICALLY

A man who had been away from God decided to surprise his mother and go back to church. When his mother walked into the church and saw him sitting in her pew, she looked up and said to everyone there, "Oh my Lord, you all better run. The ceiling is going to fall in! My son has come to church today!" She wanted to be cute and funny in encouraging her son, but it humiliated him.

I want to encourage you to affirm your prodigal specifically. Ask God for wisdom about what you might say. Look hard for things your prodigal does well. For instance:

- If he's a good golfer, talk to him about his latest round and tell him he's terrific.
- If she has gotten a promotion at work, tell her how proud you are of her.
- If your son takes his children to the zoo, tell him how much you appreciate his attention and love for his kids.
- If your daughter volunteers at the hospital, tell her you are impressed with her kindness.
- If she prepared dinner, tell her she's a wonderful cook.
- If your son repaired his car, compliment him on his ingenuity.

Focus on the things your prodigal enjoys. Do not use affirmation as a wedge to get close enough to pounce and say something corrective. Speak affirming words clearly and avoid any subtle jabs.

DON'T CRITICIZE YOUR CHURCH

Sometimes parents are critical of the very people God uses to bring His grace into the life of the prodigal. I talked to a young man who had gotten far from God. He desperately wanted to find some common ground with his dad, a staff member at a large church. The son spent time with another man in the church who, unknown to the dad, was gently showing him the love of Christ and answering his many questions. I told this young man I would pray that he and his father would find reconciliation.

A few weeks later, I was at the church to speak. That night, while the three of us were eating dinner together, the father verbally berated the son's new friend. He said that the man was ungodly and selfish because he did not support a raise for the staff at the last finance committee meeting. I watched the father destroy in five minutes all that God had been doing to bring light into this young man's heart.

You may be angry at your pastor, but do not call him names around your prodigal. You may not like the music that was played last Sunday, but do not complain just because it was not to your personal tastes.

You may be angry at God, but take it up with someone who can help you reason through your anger. Avoid someone who has his own issues with God.

The people and functions of your church may be the very tools God is using to bring your prodigal back to Himself. Do not let your critical words postpone God's work in his life.

SOWING AND REAPING

The law of sowing and reaping operates in every area of our lives, including the words we use and how we use them. When we sow seeds of criticism, we reap a harvest of bitterness. When we sow condemnation, we reap distance. When we sow seeds of love and affirmation, the harvest is one of hope and acceptance.

Are your words seeds of hope or despair in the heart of your prodigal? You are making an impact one way or the other. I encourage you to try two experiments. First, ask ten people for an analysis of how you communicate with your prodigal or about your prodigal. Most of them will probably tell you only what they think you want to hear, unless you assure them that you want their frank, honest answers. Ask your volunteers to remind you of specific times when they overheard you say things to your prodigal. Ask them about times when you spoke about your prodigal to them. Do not defend yourself. Listen to what they say, and ask follow-up questions such as, "How do you think that made her feel when I said that?" or "Did that statement make you think less of my son?"

The second experiment is more significant. Ask your prodigal to tell you what messages you communicated to him in the past. Your prodigal may not want to incur more criticism. You should expect him to be very reluctant to respond. Assure him that you will not argue and that you will listen carefully to whatever he says. You may find that some of the messages you thought were most hurtful did not have much impact. You may also find that messages you thought were minor caused a lot of pain.

Use these two experiments as opportunities for repentance. If you discover that your words have sown seeds of hurt, ask for forgiveness. From this moment on, determine to speak only words that edify.

Do you remember the encouragement Paul gave to the Ephesian believers? He told them, "Let no corrupt word proceed out of your mouth, but what is good for necessary edification, that it may impart grace to the hearers" (Eph. 4:29). In other words, stop letting your words tear people down, and be sure they build people up instead. No matter what it takes, do it. Repentance is a courageous and continuous act. Trust God for wisdom and power to fulfill His calling to be a healer with your words.

Words are important, but we also need to remember that studies show that 93 percent of communication is nonverbal. The vast majority of what we communicate to others is found in our facial expressions and gestures. If you say, "I love you" with a warm smile and outreached arms, the message rings true. If you say the same words with a scowl on your face and your arms crossed, the recipient doubts your sincerity.

Some of us force ourselves to say the right words. Our prodigals, however, see contradictions communicated on our faces and in our body language. They can tell if our words are genuine. Insincere words take you a step backward. We build trust only when words are real.

Think about the nonverbal messages that accompany the words you speak. Do you roll your eyes? Do you turn your back? Do you scowl or wince? Your body language is very important. Become a student of it. Learn, change, and grow.

BE PATIENT

Jesus used agrarian metaphors not only because most people were farmers but because they communicate realities of life very effectively. A farmer does not plant today and expect a harvest tomorrow. The growing cycle requires lots of time. A wise farmer is both careful and patient. He plows and prepares the ground in the spring. He plants seeds and then prays for good weather as they begin to sprout. If he gets good weather, he harvests in summer or fall.

Not only do we reap what we sow, but we find other parallels between sowing seeds of grain and sowing seeds of love in the lives of our prodigals. For example, we should not expect a prodigal to change simply because we speak one kind word after years of criticism. Just as hard earth must be plowed before it is conducive for the growth of seeds, a hard heart must be softened before it is receptive to seeds of hope. It is far more realistic to speak positive words over a long period before we expect any results.

We need to "plow" our own hearts to prepare them. Allow God to work through us with compassion rather than criticism. Then, as we sow seeds of love in the hearts of our prodigals, we need to wait patiently for those seeds to take root. Many of our prodigals become skeptical of kind words. They wonder if we will go back to our old habits of nagging and condemning.

Many of our prodigals will wait to see if we really mean what we say. If we are consistent in expressing love, they may respond with joy and thankfulness. But since they are usually resistant to change, they will not necessarily repent of their sins on the spot. The prostitutes and tax collectors who gathered around Jesus did not comprehend His message right away. They did feel His love and wanted to be near Him. As they spent time with Him, His grace and truth rubbed off on them.

Some studies indicate that it takes fourteen affirming

statements to overcome a single negative one. Many parents reverse this ratio. If we want our prodigals to listen, we must use correction only when it is accompanied by grace and love, expressed both verbally and nonverbally.

BE ACCOUNTABLE

Changing years of bad habits is not easy. We need wisdom, courage, and others who care enough to hold us accountable. Your spouse, a good friend, or your pastor may be able to fulfill that crucial role for you. Ask the person to give you a signal (a hand motion or a simple word) to let you know when you are off-base again in conversations with your prodigal. Invite that person to speak honestly to help you uncover motives and emotions that drive your actions. Deal with your hurts and disappointments. Address your anger and humiliation. As God works deep in your heart, your perspective will gradually change and your messages to your prodigal will change too. During this time of reflection, determine to speak words of kindness no matter how you feel. It is right. It is good. It pleases God.

KINDNESS IS A CHOICE

Some parents challenge me: "What if I do not feel like saying affirming things to my prodigal? If I say them anyway, isn't that hypocrisy? Phil, you know how Jesus felt about hypocrites. I sure don't want to be one of them!"

It is certainly laudable to avoid hypocrisy. But God calls us to obey Him even when we do not feel like it. Jesus pleaded with the Father to let Him escape the horror of the cross. His prayer was so intense that sweat fell from His brow like drops of blood. He knew the intense pain He would experience, but He still submitted to the Father's will. I believe it is the Father's will that family members speak words of grace to their prodigals, even when they do not feel like it. The commands in Scripture are clear. We are to be tenderhearted and speak only those words that build up.

Kindness is a choice. It is not a feeling. If you feel angry, take your anger to God and let Him give you insight and healing. Do not let your anger be an excuse for withdrawing or condemning. Choose to do what God commands.

Richard often disappointed his mom, who often communicated her disappointment in words, facial expressions, and body language. After I talked with her, she accepted my challenge to speak words of grace to him.

She was still angry at him for foolish decisions and gambling away his money. She determined, however, to start affirming him. She prayed and asked God to show her something that he did well. A few things came to mind: his diligence at work, his beautiful rosebushes, and the way he helped her when her old car needed repairs. She also realized she needed to stop nagging him about not coming to church, his frequent trips to the dog track, his choice of friends, and the way he treated his ex-wife and kids. She determined to bite her tongue about those things and focus on the good.

She started with, "Richard, I appreciate all your hard work at the office. I'm sure you're doing a good job there." To be honest, her words sounded as contrived to her as they sounded foreign to him. In the past she'd complained about him spending so much time at work. He did not know how to take this unexpected compliment, so he mumbled, "Thanks."

A few days later, she commented, "I hope your roses will be as pretty this year as they were last year." Again, Richard expected this to be only a ploy to start a conversation so she could drop verbal bombs about his gambling, but she did not.

Months went by as she stuck to using only positive comments. She told me, "I'm not sure if the change affected him, but it sure affected me! When I stopped dwelling on his faults, I felt freer and more relaxed. And believe it or not, I actually enjoyed seeing him again."

After several more months, the plowing, sowing, watering, and waiting finally bore fruit in Richard's life. One day he told her, "Mom, I don't know what happened, but you've definitely changed. At first I thought you were putting me on. I didn't believe you appreciated anything about me. But I guess you do."

His mother's eyes filled with tears as he continued, "Mom, why don't you come over and help me cut some roses? I think they'd look good on your dining room table."

Richard did not stop gambling that day. He did not come back to church that next Sunday. He and his mother, though, began a new chapter in their relationship. It was one based on respect, kindness, and love.

About a year later, someone sat down beside her in church during the first hymn. She turned and saw Richard smiling at her. He'd chosen to be in church with her instead of going to the track. *Glory to God!* she thought.

- -

TRUTH TO REMEMBER

Words impact your prodigal. Choose them carefully.

- -

Chapter 9

· · · — — · · ·

PRINCIPLE SIX: PRAYING THE HARD PRAYERS

"PHIL, I'VE PRAYED for my son every day for his entire life, for fifty-three years now. I enjoyed praying for him while he was in school. When he joined the navy and got involved in drinking, I prayed even harder. During the last twenty-five years, I've prayed over and over again for God to change his heart, but nothing has happened. I still pray, Phil, but now they're just words. I've stopped expecting an answer."

Many family members can identify with this mother. She is a devout Christian who loves God with all her heart. She, however, cannot understand why God does not answer her prayers. She praised God when her son told her he stopped drinking. Then he started again. She thanked the

Father for His mercy when her son came back to church. Then he quit.

"I'm about prayed out, Phil," she almost whispered.

People struggle to hang on to their faith. In the gospel of Mark, there is a confrontation between Jesus and the father of a demon-possessed boy:

> Then they brought [the boy] to Him. And when he saw Him, immediately the spirit convulsed him, and he fell on the ground and wallowed, foaming at the mouth.
>
> So He asked his father, "How long has this been happening to him?"
>
> And he said, "From childhood. And often he has thrown him both into the fire and into the water to destroy him. But if You can do anything, have compassion on us and help us."
>
> Jesus said to him, "If you can believe, all things are possible to him who believes."
>
> Immediately the father of the child cried out and said with tears, "Lord, I believe; help my unbelief!"
>
> When Jesus saw that the people came running together, He rebuked the unclean spirit, saying to it: "Deaf and dumb spirit, I command you, come out of him and enter him no more!" Then the spirit cried out, convulsed him greatly, and came out of

him. And he became as one dead, so that many said, "He is dead." But Jesus took him by the hand and lifted him up, and he arose. (9:20–27)

Family members of prodigals sometimes feel the frustration of the father in this story. They tried everything. They prayed for years. They believe in God. Now their faith has waivered. They no longer believe God is going to work in their prodigals' hearts.

I want to encourage you to be honest about your struggles with unbelief, just like the father was honest with Jesus. Words of encouragement: You cannot give up. Keep trusting our merciful Lord to accomplish His purposes. Let me offer some specific prayers to help you pray.

"LORD, USE MY PRODIGAL'S FRIENDS"

In my conversations with prodigals who returned to the Lord, I asked, "Who had the greatest influence to convince you to turn back to Christ?" To my surprise, it was not their parents or siblings. The primary positive influence on prodigals was their friends who cared enough to speak the truth and took them to church.

A prodigal expects his parents to push him toward God. He, however, often disregards them as an influence. On the other hand, a coworker, a friend, a neighbor, or someone who is a member of the same club can often find a prodigal's listening ear, which has been closed to parents.

My encouragement, then, is for parents to pray, "Lord, would You bring a godly friend into my prodigal's life to share the message of hope and model a life of trust in You? Bring somebody who will love my prodigal with Your love and melt his heart with Your grace."

When your prodigal tells you that she went to another church with a friend, do not give her a lecture about how she should have come to your church. A friend of mine prayed diligently for twenty years that his son would get right with God. In answer to his prayers, God worked in the son's life. A coworker shared the gospel with him. As a result, he became a Christian. The son started attending an Assembly of God church with his coworker. He really grew in his faith.

But my friend, the boy's father, attends a Baptist church. He took his son aside and scolded him: "Son, I'm ashamed of you! How could you go to an Assembly of God church when you know I disapprove of the way they do things?" I am sure the Son of God rejoiced that the man's son had come to faith. The father, however, had a different agenda. Being a Baptist, it appeared, was more important to him than being a Christian.

When this son told me this story, I could tell he was heartbroken by his father's harsh words. I gave him a hug and told him, "My friend, your dad is wrong about this. I'm so proud of you for walking with God. And I'm thrilled that God has led you to a church where you are being encouraged in your faith. Maybe someday your dad will understand this too."

Some parents try to put the squeeze on their kids if they attend a different church while they are still searching for God. Sometimes I hear, "Phil, we need my son at our church. I don't know why he'd go to that other one."

Do not get your priorities mixed up. The condition of your prodigal's heart is a greater concern to God than which pew supports the seat of his pants. If God uses another Bible-believing church down the street to influence your prodigal for the kingdom, be glad for him.

Please do not interfere with the work of God in your prodigal's life. Rejoice that your prodigal is interested enough to go to church anywhere at all! Thank God for your prodigal's friend, no matter what evangelical church he attends.

If you have the opportunity, make a point of thanking the friend for being an answer to prayer. Thank him for letting God use him to be such a positive influence on your prodigal. Do not make a big deal of it. You may not even want your prodigal to know you are thanking the other person. Let the friend know you will keep praying for both him and your prodigal as they walk with God together.

"LORD, CHANGE ME FIRST"

Earlier in these pages, I mentioned the need for us to look inside our own hearts to address the resentment and disappointment that are a part of having a prodigal. It is easier to focus on all the changes our prodigals need to make. We need, though, to begin by praying, "Lord, work in my heart. Even if the prodigal I love never changes, change me."

David and the other psalmists expressed their hearts openly to God. They did not sugarcoat how they felt. They were painfully honest and direct in addressing God. Many of the psalms express deep disappointment and heartache. David wrote,

> How long, O Lord? Will You forget me forever?
> How long will You hide Your face from me?
> (Ps. 13:1)

As the psalmists were honest with God, He met them at their deepest point of need. He reminded them of His goodness and sovereignty. The psalms almost always end with expressions of hope and trust. After David poured out his anguish to God, he found refreshment in God's wisdom and love. See how he finished the psalm:

> But I have trusted in Your mercy;
> My heart shall rejoice in Your salvation.

I will sing to the LORD,
Because He has dealt bountifully with me.
(Ps. 13:5–6)

Most of us pray for years that God will change our prodigals. Perhaps we need to pray that God will change us first. Perhaps God wants to work on our bitterness. Maybe God wants to ease our pain by having us confront our grief and disappointment. Maybe God wants to deflate our sense of self-righteousness and remind us that He is God, not us. Maybe God wants to replace our hopelessness with joy and thankfulness.

Our prodigals need the touch of God, but we need to feel it first. Then, as God works His kindness and healing in our hearts, our lives can better reflect God's love to our prodigals.

"LORD, GIVE ME A FRESH PERSPECTIVE"

We often quote Romans 8:28, but do we really believe that "all things work together for good to those who love God, to those who are the called according to His purpose"? We wish God would answer our prayers and fix things. We wish our prodigals would repent and our families would be united in peace and love. That's how we would work things together for good, is it not?

God's ways often are full of irony. I believe that His

purpose is not necessarily to make our lives happy. It is to do whatever it takes to get us to trust Him. Our pains and failures are tools in His hands as they turn our thoughts toward Him. C. S. Lewis called pain "God's megaphone" to get our attention. Instead of trying to avoid pain at all costs and whining when we cannot get our prayers answered, we can ask God for a fresh perspective.

The pains we experience highlight our need for God. The longing we have for a prodigal to return to God is the very thing that makes us depend on Him. When we are weak, our faith can become strong. Foolish things our prodigals do embarrass us. Yet that foolishness is an opportunity for God's wisdom and power to shine. In the midst of all the darkness, God may even choose to use you and me to bring His light to someone we love.

Rather than becoming obsessed with the evil around you, ask God to give you a fresh perspective. Ask Him to help you see how He can bring good out of it. Look for the hand of God in your difficult situations. He is willing to use even the most horrible sins and the most foolish choices, as long as we trust Him to do it.

"LORD, I ASK FOR BROKENNESS"

It is a dictum of Alcoholics Anonymous that a person has to "hit rock bottom" in order to change. We are prideful people.

We do not want to admit our needs. We try to compensate for our shortcomings any way we can. Your prodigal is no different. She will cling to any hope of fooling herself, her friends, and her family as long as she can.

Most prodigals do not look for help until they become very needy. In fact, as I watch people in trouble, the only factor that determines whether someone gets help is utter desperation. When people become desperate, they will cling to anything that promises the hope of change. Before they reach that point, however, they use all kinds of excuses and mind games to convince themselves that they are doing fine.

Jack has a sister who is an alcoholic. He started sharing Christ with her while she was in high school. She never listened. She made fun of him to her friends, but nothing could stop him from loving her.

They are now in their forties. He still prays for her every day. He asks God to touch her heart, break through the hard shell of her pride, and draw her to Himself. He prays for her brokenness.

Through four failed marriages, two miscarriages, a bout with cancer, and a near-fatal car accident, she remains unbroken. In each case, people told her, "Wow! You are so unlucky! Look at all the bad things that have happened to you." My friend believes God is answering his prayers. Each calamity has brought an opportunity for her to "come to her senses" and repent. Each heartache is God's megaphone to get her attention. So far, she is not responding.

"I don't know what it's going to take for God to get through to her," Jack told me sadly. "But there's one thing I'm sure of: God is sure doing His job of giving her chances to repent. I couldn't ask Him to be any clearer in showing her the desperate need in her life. Maybe someday she'll listen."

Before we feel sorry for the hard times our prodigals go through, maybe we should ask, "God, is this Your way of getting his attention?" If it is, then we must avoid trying to fix their problems. Instead, we need to let God have His way in our prodigals' lives.

"LORD, HELP ME FIGHT THE BATTLE"

Make no mistake: You and I are in a spiritual battle all day every day. The forces of evil are strong. They are nothing compared to the incredible power of God. Our prodigals may be in the grip of evil, but God is far stronger.

We Christians tend to make one of two mistakes when thinking about the devil. We either do not think about him enough or we think he has more power than he actually does. We know he is a thief who comes "to steal, and to kill, and to destroy" (John 10:10). He delights in deceiving our prodigals about the goodness of God. He delights in deceiving us about God's gracious intentions. He knows that if he gets us to question God's character, he gains a foothold to exploit.

We resist him with truth and grace, with the Word of God, and with the power of love. Paul reminds us:

> [God] raised [Jesus] from the dead and seated Him at His right hand in the heavenly places, far above all principality and power and might and dominion, and every name that is named, not only in this age but also in that which is to come.
>
> And He put all things under His feet, and gave Him to be head over all things to the church, which is His body, the fullness of Him who fills all in all. (Eph. 1:20–23)

Jesus is not "barely" above the forces of darkness. He is "far" above them. He is infinitely more powerful. He gives us tremendous resources for the battle we fight. Later in the same letter, Paul instructs us to fight and to use all the armor available to us (Eph. 6:10–20). Soldiers in battle expect to get dirty. Wounds are expected. If a soldier's resources are good and their commander is a great leader, however, they are confident of victory.

When you pray hard for changes yet nothing happens, you are in good company. The prophet Daniel once prayed for three weeks for God's help. Finally, the angel Michael appeared. He explained that God had heard his prayer the first time he uttered it, but an adversary blocked the path of the help God had sent.

God hears every prayer, but Satan remains active in attempting to block God's good work. Prayers is essential for your victory. They are vital for the successful return of your prodigal. Ask God to give you a fresh perspective on spiritual conflict so you can fight effectively for your prodigal.

"LORD, DON'T LET ME GIVE UP"

Some of us want to just give up. We have had it. We tried being nice. We tried being tough. We listened to the advice of friends. We prayed a million times for our prodigals to change. Still, nothing changes.

The fruit of the Spirit includes the quality of "longsuffering." Tenacity is one of the primary virtues in the Christian life. The Bible urges us to "run with endurance the race that is set before us" (Heb. 12:1).

People who run marathons tell me that at various times in the race, they want to quit. Their legs feel like lead. Their stomachs ache. Their vision gets blurry. They even become nauseated. They feel like they cannot take another step, but they take that one . . . and the next.

The Christian life is similar. It's a marathon, not a sprint. Jesus is our supreme example of tenacity. Scripture encourages us to keep "looking unto Jesus, the author and finisher of our faith, who for the joy that was set before Him endured the cross, despising the shame" (Heb. 12:2). Jesus could endure the worst that life offered because He knew what would come later: resurrection and reunion with the Father. As we follow His example, we need tenacity to keep going, to keep believing that God is good and that He is sovereign. Even when we see no visible evidence, we can trust His Word that He is at work.

"LORD, WHATEVER IT TAKES . . ."

While our eyes are on Jesus and His supreme example of sacrifice, we begin to see the value of brokenness. Parents need to be willing to pray, "Lord, I will do whatever it takes for my prodigal to respond to You." In Paul's letter to the Romans, he expressed a passionate hope for his kinsmen's salvation:

> I tell the truth in Christ, I am not lying, my conscience also bearing me witness in the Holy Spirit, that I have great sorrow and continual grief in my heart. For I could wish that I myself were accursed from Christ for my brethren, my countrymen according to the flesh. (9:1–3)

I think this sounds like the desperate plea of someone who loves a prodigal. Paul speculated about going to hell if that act could achieve salvation for the people he loved. No sacrifice was too great, including the exchange of his own salvation for theirs. Can you say the same about your commitment to your prodigal?

I grew up in a solid, secure family as an only child. We had none of those "dysfunctional family" problems you hear so much about these days. My parents were very loving. I was a happy kid. As a boy, our family attended my mother's home church. She was one of eleven children, and with the exception of one brother, all of her siblings attended that same church.

My mother's oldest brother is Charlie, nicknamed Bud. Uncle Bud was quite a bit older than my mom. He was a godly man who loved to pray. When I went into the ministry, I had an office behind my house, and Uncle Bud often stopped in to see me. Sometimes he would say, "Phil, I need us to pray about something. Will you pray with me?" I enjoyed those times praying together.

One time he told me through tears that one of his grandchildren had a brain tumor. I knew Uncle Bud was serious about prayer when he wanted to kneel. He was crippled in one of his legs, making it quite an ordeal for him to get on his knees. That was, however, the desired position for the kind of praying Uncle Bud wanted to do. We prayed for his grandson that day. God miraculously spared his life. Uncle Bud came by a couple of other times when there was conflict in the church. He did not want my advice. He just wanted me to pray with him.

One day Uncle Bud came by for a casual visit. As we talked, the conversation turned more serious. He told me he had four children who were all walking with the Lord. Some of his grandchildren, though, were not. It broke his heart. He loved those young people. He wept as he talked about their lives. They were doing some things that would embarrass other parents or grandparents and evoke sharp criticism. Uncle Bud never criticized them. He just loved them. We knelt and prayed that day for his grandchildren.

One of them was Marla, who had walked away from the Lord while in college. After graduation, Uncle Bud (Marla's grandfather) got very sick with cancer. During his illness, he kept loving Marla and showing great kindness to her. His love melted her heart. She came back to God.

One day in a chapel service, Marla gave her testimony and shared how that special man had loved her. He prayed for her when others criticized her. He smiled when others frowned. As he lay dying of cancer, she remembered that he didn't talk about himself. When she went to see him, he only wanted to talk about her life and what interested her. God touched her heart through her sick grandfather.

Marla blessed the name of God with her story.

That afternoon when I left the office, I glanced over to where my old office was when Uncle Bud was alive. I remembered his prayers for her. At that moment, I prayed, "Lord, if You see uncle Bud walking around heaven today, would You tell him that his Marla blessed Your name today? I think he'd enjoy hearing about that. Tell him his prayers have been answered."

You've read this far into the book, so you are obviously committed to loving your prodigal. You probably are praying for your prodigal as Charlie prayed for Marla. I wish I could guarantee that your prodigal will respond. I wish I could give you a formula that is sure to work, but I cannot. What we can do is say to God, "Lord, I want to be an instrument to do all I can to bring my child back to You. I'm willing to live, and I'm willing to die. I'm willing to be rich or to be poor. I'm willing to live in pain if that's what it takes for You to work deeply in my life and pour out Your love on my child. I'm Yours, Lord. Do whatever it takes."

After you are gone, you may be walking around heaven when you hear the Lord say, "I've got great news. Your prodigal has come home!" What a wonderful day that will be!

- -

TRUTH TO REMEMBER

Ask God to give your prodigal godly friends and to use anything necessary to get your prodigal's attention.

- -

Chapter 10

· · · — — · · ·

HOPING FOR THE END OF THE JOURNEY

NANCY STOOD with her daughter, Christy, as she told me about her relationship with her forty-five-year-old son, Rob. "I loved him so much that I closed my eyes to all he was doing wrong. When I finally saw things clearly, I hated him. He was a mess. So was I. As a boy, he was the 'golden child,' cute and funny. Everybody said he had the most wonderful personality, and they were right. I guess we bragged on him too often . . ." Nancy's voice trailed off for a moment. Then she continued. "It really went to his head. By the time he graduated from high school, he thought he was the center of the universe. I guess he was, in our family at least."

Christy added, "I sure loved my older brother. Rob was so handsome. He looked just like Elvis, even in high school. The girls thought he was the cutest! We had a lot of fun together. We teased each other all the time, and for a little sister, that was something special. And Rob was really protective. I never had to worry about guys treating me badly. A time or two, Rob followed through with his threats to protect me. I'll tell you, that sure made an impression on me—and on everybody else at the school. I loved him so much."

Nancy then told me the reason she was talking to me. "After Rob graduated from high school, he was so self-centered that everybody and everything had to revolve around him. He got married, but when his wife didn't worship him—well, the way Christy and I did—he divorced her. He married somebody else and soon divorced her for the same reason. Over a period of fifteen years, he got married six times, but three of those marriages were to the same woman. I guess she kept thinking things would change. They didn't."

Nancy stared at the ceiling a few seconds before continuing. "As a boy, we never wanted him to be unhappy. We gave him whatever he wanted, so Rob never developed an ability to handle money. By his second or third marriage, he was also in trouble financially. He started a business, which—I heard from a reliable source—he burned down so he could collect the insurance. The police suspected him, but he got away with it. He started gambling to try to make a lot of money fast. He won sometimes and then felt as if he were on top of the world, but far more often he lost everything he had at the blackjack table."

Another pause, and Nancy continued, "Did I mention that he beat his wives? It's remarkable that one woman went back to him for the third time. It looks like I raised a monster, doesn't it? But I couldn't see it. I told myself for years and years that all his problems were somebody else's fault. I tried my best to help him. I gave him advice about the women he was going with, but he married them anyway. I would ask him to come over and fix something at my house when I knew he was planning to go to the casino, but he caught on and stopped coming.

"He only came to church when he was scared to death about something, like when one of his wives asked for a restraining order or when he thought he'd had a heart attack. At one point, he had two sons born during the same week— one from a previous wife and the other with his current wife. So he didn't want to talk to me about anything having to do with God."

Nancy now spoke in somber tones. "As I look back, he was domineering even as a boy. I overlooked it because he was so smart and good-looking. But when something didn't go his way, he pouted or threw a tantrum or something. Christy was the first to see the problems developing, but when she tried to talk to me, I wouldn't hear a word of it. I thought she was betraying Rob by saying bad things about him. I hate to say it, but it literally took me years to wipe away the scales and see the truth. Rob is a selfish, hard-hearted, violent bum. And when I finally saw the truth, I hated him. For many years I was enraged at him, but I also felt ashamed. I couldn't believe he was so selfish, and I couldn't believe I had helped produce that monster."

Christy gave her mother a hug as Nancy told how she had found some peace. "I stopped talking to Rob for a long time. I refused to go to one of his weddings, and I sure didn't want to get involved in any of his problems anymore. I was furious. Christy had been trying to help Rob, but she realized long before I did that trying to control him wasn't helping him or us. When she stopped, I first thought she was being selfish, but as time went on, I saw she was right. Blindness had been my problem for years, followed by a long period of bitterness. I desperately needed some peace. Christy helped me learn to forgive Rob, to stop fixing his problems, and to love him without expecting anything in return. It's been hard, but God has forgiven me for treating Rob like an idol, and Christy has forgiven me for preferring him over her when she was little. All I can do now is live each day trusting God to give me wisdom and joy, and that's exactly what I'm doing. Rob hasn't changed, but I have. I now have joy in my life that I never had before, and it's wonderful!"

Nancy and Christy embraced like two war veterans at a reunion. They'd faced bullets of anger, hurt, and manipulation. And they had come through the fight together.

Parents of prodigals can seek two joys. One is God's response to their faithfulness. The other is the possible return of their prodigals. Let's look at those joys.

THE JOY OF OUR FAITHFULNESS

Nancy understood and experienced the first of these two joys. When we are following Christ and doing what He wants us to do, it pleases Him. The day will come when you and I stand before Christ and He will ask us about our lives as believers. Paul described this event in his first letter to the Corinthians. Our deeds as believers will pass through the flame of judgment. Those done for selfish reasons will burn, but those done for Christ's glory will endure and be rewarded. Paul wrote,

> Each one's work will become clear; for the Day will declare it, because it will be revealed by fire; and the fire will test each one's work, of what sort it is. If anyone's work which he has built on it endures, he will receive a reward. If anyone's work is burned, he will suffer loss; but he himself will be saved, yet so as through fire. (3:13–15)

On that day, God will look at our hearts and our faithfulness. He will not ask you and me about our prodigals. He will be seeing our perseverance to trust Him even when our prodigals did not come home. If we are faithful, we will hear those wonderful words, "Well done, good and faithful servant . . . Enter into the joy of your master" (Matt. 25:21 ESV). We all long to hear those words.

Our Lord will evaluate our obedience.

Did we trust God and speak truth?

Did we stop withdrawing and move toward our prodigals in strong love?

Did we look for what we could affirm instead of what we so easily condemned?

Did we make the hard choice to thank God even when things looked bleak?

Did we keep praying even when we saw no answers?

Did we help other parents of prodigals who were struggling to find hope and meaning?

None of us does these things perfectly, yet as we practice we get a lot more consistent.

To remain faithful, family members of prodigals need the strong hope that God will accomplish His purposes, even if His purposes are not like ours and are on His timetable rather than ours. Our hope cannot depend on the responses of our prodigals. It must be founded on the character of God Himself.

Psalm 130 contains a beautiful description of this kind of hope. The psalmist compared his trust in God to a lookout on the wall of a besieged city. The greatest danger occured during the night when the enemy could sneak up close to the walls. The lookout peered intently into the darkness, watching and longing to see that first ray of light in the east that meant day was coming and he would be able to see far more clearly. The psalmist wrote:

> I wait for the LORD, my soul waits,
> And in His word I do hope.
> My soul waits for the Lord
> More than those who watch for the morning—
> Yes, more than those who watch for the morning.
> (Ps. 130:5–6)

In the Scriptures, the idea of "waiting" implies a strong hope. It is an expectation that something will happen. We "wait for the bus" not simply because we hope it will come, but because we have witnessed it coming and have grown to count on it to be there at its scheduled time. We "wait on God" because we know that we can trust the consistency of His faithfulness and character. Sometimes we wish God had a schedule we could follow. In fact, God's schedule is often slow from our perspective. Yet we can be certain that He will, eventually, come.

In the meantime, our souls wait in eager expectation for the God of the Universe, the One who is both good and sovereign, to shine His light on our hearts. Like a lookout on the city walls, we may be under attack and in the darkness, but we can trust that God will soon enough provide the light we need. It takes great faith to wait for the Lord. Even our expectation that He will bring light sooner or later is evidence of our trust in His goodness and grace.

Another encouraging passage is Jeremiah's statement of confidence in Lamentations. Jeremiah was surrounded by prodigals! The entire nation of Israel was a prodigal country, but the prophet riveted his eyes on God's grace, and he found peace there. He prayed:

> Remember my affliction and roaming,
> The wormwood and the gall.
> My soul still remembers
> And sinks within me.
> This I recall to my mind,
> Therefore I have hope.
> Through the LORD's mercies we are not consumed,
> Because His compassions fail not.
> They are new every morning;
> Great is Your faithfulness.
> "The LORD is my portion," says my soul,
> "Therefore I hope in Him!"
> The LORD is good to those who wait for Him,
> To the soul who seeks Him.

It is good that one should hope and wait quietly
For the salvation of the LORD. (Lam. 3:19–26)

Jeremiah did not sugarcoat his predicament. He experienced affliction, bitterness, and gall. Disappointment filled his heart. He refused to wallow in hopelessness. Instead of it consuming him, he chose to focus on God's love and faithfulness, which was "new every morning." He waited expectantly, hoping that the God who is far above all would meet him in the quietness of his heart.

Jeremiah is a model for us to remain faithful in hope. His experience was dark and foreboding. He trusted God. In the same way, being the parent of a prodigal is often a bleak venture. We, too, can trust God. We do not know if our prodigals will repent. We do not know if they will ever change, but we can. We can remain faithful even when those around us are faithless.

Your prodigal will have to account for his own choices before God's throne. God will not hold his or her mistakes against you. Instead, the Lord will look at you and ask, "Did you trust Me? Did you love the unlovable and forgive the deep hurts you experienced? Did you reach out? Did you treat your prodigal like an adult instead of like a child, expecting him to act responsibly?"

God does not expect perfection. He only desires honesty,

a contrite heart, and a willingness to progress in our relationships. If we take steps to obey Him, we will hear those wonderful words, "Well done, good and faithful servant."

THE JOY OF THEIR REPENTANCE

Some prodigals never return. Some come back for good.
Some return for a while, to the joy of their parents, but return
to the "far country" and leave their parents weeping again.

We cannot force a prodigal to repent. The best we can
do is to act like the father in Jesus' story and long for the
prodigal's return. If we see him coming down that long road
toward home, we can run to embrace him and let the celebration begin!

God is willing to use every situation, no matter how
tragic, to bring reconciliation between prodigals and their
parents.

Rachel became pregnant in high school. Her father, full
of shame, forced her to leave his house. She gave birth to a
little boy whom she named Johnny, but her father refused to
see either one of them. When the rift between her and her
father failed to heal, Rachel moved to a city several hours
away. Through the next twelve years, her mother maintained
contact, but her father remained estranged. Time only deep-
ened his bitterness and shame.

One day her mother called Rachel to say that her dad had
been in a terrible car accident. He was in the hospital, near

death. She wanted to go to his bedside but knew she was the last person on earth he wanted to see. To her surprise, her mother told her, "Rachel, your father wants to see you . . . and Johnny. Can you come?"

She and her almost-teenager jumped in her car and sped across the state to the hospital. As they approached her father's room in the ICU, she swallowed hard and knocked on the door. Her mother's voice said, "Come in." Rachel went in and saw her father with tubes in his chest and wires hooked up all over his body. Her mother smiled and motioned for them to come to his bedside. Her father smiled as he reached out and touched her hand. Tears streamed down his face, then hers and her mother's. Her father tried to speak, but Rachel told him, "Not now, Daddy. You can tell me later."

He shook his head. "No," he whispered, "this has taken way too long already. Rachel, I'm so sorry. Will you please forgive me for being so unkind to you and Johnny?"

Rachel wept as she nodded her acceptance of his apology. Through her sobs, she told him, "Daddy, I was wrong too. Will you forgive me for getting pregnant?"

The sobs of joy were so loud that a nurse burst into the room to see what was wrong. "Nothing's wrong," Rachel's mother told her. "We're a family again." The nurse smiled as she backed out of the room.

God uses all kinds of things to bring families back

together. Sometimes He uses the broken hearts of the prodigals. Sometimes He uses the broken hearts of the parents. Sometimes He uses tragedies to mend hearts and homes. I know that God is very much at work to give us opportunities to respond to Him. Rachel's father's heart remained hardened until he faced death. At that moment, God melted his resistance and he reached out to his daughter and grandson. Reconciliation began.

Throughout this book are stories of prodigals. As I think back on scores of conversations with men and women who turned their backs on God, I can see the faces of many who have come home. But I also remember the faces of those who, for whatever reason, chose to stay in the hog pen, hungry and alone.

When the prodigal son returned, his father ordered the servants to put the best robe on his shoulders, a ring on his hand, and sandals on his feet. He killed the fattened calf and prepared a great feast, "for this my son was dead and is alive again; he was lost and is found" (Luke 15:24).

It bears repeating that each of these items symbolized the father's acceptance of his son. The robe was for important guests. It signified dignity. The son smelled like the hogs he had been feeding, but the father immediately bestowed dignity on the one who had none.

The ring was a symbol of authority, of sonship restored. This young man had wasted every possession and every cent of his inheritance. In coming home, his only desire was to be a hired servant under his father's roof. His father returned him to a place of prominence as his dear son.

The sandals signify status. Only slaves and servants went barefooted, as the young man probably was when his father embraced him. The boy expected to remain unshod as a hired servant, but the father ordered that the sandals of status be given to him.

The fattened calf was for only the most important celebrations. The father saw his son's return as the greatest blessing he could experience. It was the answer to his prayers all those years his son was away. Now it was time to celebrate. No expense was too great. Joy overflowed from the father's heart during this most special occasion of all.

If your prodigal returns, do not spare the joy—experience it in its fullness. Do not remind him of the stupid things he did while he was away. Do not beat yourself up for not being the parent you should have been. Live in the joyous present, not in the shameful past. Follow the father's example, and give wonderful gifts of love to show your acceptance to your returning prodigal.

Your prodigal's repentance is the beginning of a journey of reconciliation. There will be adjustments to be made on both sides. The relationship cannot go back to the way it was before, but it can become better than ever. You will have more insight into yourself, your prodigal, and God's faithfulness. Your returning prodigal should appreciate your love now more than ever.

As you show care consistently, any doubts your prodigal has about the sincerity of your love will disappear. The first days and weeks may be awkward. They were for the prodigal son's elder brother. Expect some tensions and misunderstandings during those first encounters. Address them calmly and deliberately, just as the father in Jesus' story addressed the anger of his older son.

Let God continue to work His goodness and grace deep into each person's life until His wisdom and joy permeate your family. Give thanks that your prodigal is home.

I think often of the ten lepers who came to Jesus for healing. He told them to go to the priest, and on the way they were healed of their disease. All ten were made well, but only one came back to thank Jesus for what He had done. "Where are the nine?" Jesus asked (Luke 17:17). Thank God often for doing what no one else could ever do, for bringing light out of darkness in your prodigal's heart.

I HOPE FOR YOU . . .

Paul and Silas were on an exciting adventure responding to Christ's command to take the gospel to the entire world. In Europe they found a woman, Lydia, who trusted Christ as her Savior. As Paul continued sharing the gospel with people, things were going as planned.

Then some men came along with a demon-possessed slave girl. The demon in this girl spoke and distracted the people who were listening. Paul cast the demon out of her. Her owners had been making money from the fortune-telling she did through her demonic powers. They were not happy with Paul and Silas, so they dragged them to the authorities. Here's what happened next:

> Then the multitude rose up together against them; and the magistrates tore off their clothes and commanded them to be beaten with rods. And when they had laid many stripes on them, they threw them into prison, commanding the jailer to keep them securely. Having received such a charge, he put them into the inner prison and fastened their feet in the stocks. (Acts 16:22–24)

This was not at all what Paul had planned. He and Silas were trying to do what God led them to do. Now they found themselves beaten and bloody in the innermost dungeon of the city prison, with their feet fastened in stocks. One choice was to complain. "God, how could You allow something like this? Being in prison can't be what You want. Get us out of here right now!" Another choice was to blame each other. Silas did not tell Paul, "If you hadn't cast that demon out of the slave girl, we'd be telling people about Jesus right now instead of being stuck in the bottom of this hole, bleeding on everything!"

Instead, Paul and Silas made a different choice:

> But at midnight Paul and Silas were praying and singing hymns to God, and the prisoners were listening to them. Suddenly there was a great earthquake, so that the foundations of the prison were shaken; and immediately all the doors were opened and everyone's chains were loosed. (vv. 25–26)

Instead of blaming anyone, Paul and Silas trusted that God's ways were far higher than they could imagine. When the situation was darkest (it was midnight in the dungeon), they held on to the hope that God is good and sovereign. Though they did not understand God's plan, they trusted that He had one, and that it was a good one. They sang hymns, prayed, and praised. They had no idea how their situation would turn out. In their case, God performed a miracle. An earthquake freed all the prisoners, and many more people came to Christ after seeing the power of God.

Family members of prodigals are, in many ways, in the same situation as Paul and Silas. They only want the best and never plan for their kids to become prodigals. They did not ask for the pain and darkness that descended on their hearts and their families. They feel trapped, stuck in a spiritual and emotional hole. Yet they, too, have a choice. They can fix-ate on what they wanted for themselves and their children. Or they can cling to the goodness and sovereignty of God, trusting that He understands. Even when confused in the darkness, they can pray, sing hymns, and praise God for His faithfulness.

That is your choice. Every day you can choose to believe God will work a miracle of hope and healing in your heart and, perhaps, in the life of your prodigal.

If so, some day you may look down that dusty road and see a familiar figure in the distance, and you'll rejoice that your prodigal has come home.

- -

TRUTH TO REMEMBER

Hope is your greatest motivation and encouragement. Never lose it.

- -

QUESTIONS FOR PERSONAL OR SMALL GROUP STUDY

. . . — — . . .

USING *REACHING YOUR PRODIGAL* IN CLASSES AND GROUPS

This book is designed for individual study, classes, small groups, or one-on-one with a friend. The most powerful way to benefit from these principles is for each person to study and apply the application questions individually, then to discuss them in a group setting.

Your church may want to conduct a class on Sunday mornings or on a weekday evening. A pastor or another skilled communicator can teach these principles over eight to twelve weeks. Of course, the nature of our relationships with our prodigals is complex and difficult, so it may take more than one time through the material for some people to grasp and apply it. That's entirely understandable and appropriate. I suggest that your church conduct these classes back to back over the course of the year. In most cases, those who go through once will want to go through it again because their first exposure will raise new questions.

The questions and exercises that follow aid reflection, application, and discussion. Order enough copies of the book for each person to have one. For couples, I strongly encourage both husband and wife to have a book so both can record their thoughts and prayers.

A recommended schedule for a class might be:

Week 1   Introduction to the material where the teacher can tell his own story, share his hopes for the group, provide books for each person, and discuss chapter 1.

Week 2   Chapter 2

Week 3   Chapter 3

Week 4   Chapter 4

Week 5   Chapter 5

Week 6   Chapter 6

Week 7   Chapter 7

Chapter 1

UNDERSTANDING YOUR PAIN

1. In what ways do you identify with the woman who wrote the letter to me at the beginning of this chapter?

2. As you think about the father in the parable of the prodigal son, what encourages you about his character and actions?

    • What are some things he did right?

    • What, if anything, did he do wrong?

    • How would you have handled the son's request for his share of the inheritance?

- What aspects of the father's attitude and actions challenge you?

3. What do you hope God will do in your life as a result of reading this book?

Chapter 2
SEEING YOUR PRODIGAL

1. How has your prodigal's behavior embarrassed you? How do you think it affects your actions and reactions?

2. As you think about the defiant behaviors of your prodigal, what are some ways you can respond with love instead of condemnation?

3. What are some ways you can make sure your home and church say "Prodigals Welcomed Here"?

Chapter 3
RESPONDING TO YOUR PRODIGAL

1. Have you responded to your prodigal's situation in any of the following ways? If so, describe your attitude and actions below for each one:

- Condemnation

- Self-blame

- Ignoring the problem

- Lies and cover-ups

- Nagging

- Attempts to fix the problem

- Quiet anguish

2. How have you tried to change the prodigals in your life? (Be specific about the words and actions you have used.)

- In what ways have these attempts been successful?

- In what ways have they driven a deeper wedge between you and the prodigal?

Chapter 4
PRINCIPLE ONE:
GETTING OVER THE GUILT

1. Have you felt guilty because you couldn't get your
    prodigal to turn back to God? Explain how you have
    felt about yourself and what you have done to try to
    overcome your guilt.

2. How does it help you to know that your prodigal is
    responsible for his or her own choices?

3. In what ways have you felt that somebody had to take
    the blame? Who have you blamed for your prodigal's
    problems?

4. Describe some of your feelings about guilt and conviction. Review this chapter, and then answer these questions:

- What does guilt feel like?

- What does conviction feel like?

- How can you tell the difference?

5. Describe some of the differences between guilt and conviction (the motivations, the goals, the effects on you and on your relationships, etc.).

6. Take a few minutes to respond to the Holy Spirit's prompting. In what ways is He showing you how you have sinned against your prodigal? Take this opportunity to confess your sin and experience God's cleansing grace.

Chapter 5
PRINCIPLE TWO:
REMOVING THE BARRIERS

1. Take time to pray and ask God to reveal to you the things you've done that have hurt your prodigal. As God brings them to your mind, write them here.

2. Have you created shattering wounds, eroding wounds, or vacuum wounds? Explain.

3. Consider the elements of preparing to ask for forgiveness. Write your own plan according to these guidelines:

   • Ask God for wisdom.

   • Prepare your opening statement and question.

- Anticipate your prodigal's response.

- Anticipate your response.

- End the conversation with grace.

5. Review the reasons we don't ask for forgiveness. Which of these are reasons you have used? What will be your first step in taking action to ask for forgiveness?

Chapter 6
PRINCIPLE THREE:
EXTENDING UNCONDITIONAL LOVE

1. Are any of the three reasons cited in this chapter for not loving prodigals true for you? Under the one(s) you have used, describe your attitude and actions, and answer how this has affected you and your relationship with your prodigal.

• Embarrassment

• Bitterness

• Habit

2. How have you seen bitterness destroy lives and relationships?

3. How have you seen love rebuild relationships?

4. Review the section in this chapter under the heading "You Cannot Give What You Don't Possess." In what ways do you need to experience more of God's love, forgiveness, and acceptance?

5. What difference will this make in how you relate to your prodigal?

6. Write out a plan for taking action by communicating:

- affirming words
- meaningful touch
- third-party compliments
- meaningful gifts
- quality time

7. What risks will you be taking if you love your prodigal unconditionally?

8. Is sibling jealousy a problem in your family? What is the "good kid" jealous about? What changes do you need to make, if any, to help resolve this problem?

Chapter 7

PRINCIPLE FOUR:
ALLOWING THE PAIN OF WRONG DECISIONS

1. Review the reasons for rescuing prodigals. In what ways
    can you relate to each of the following?

    • Your prodigal's failures make you look bad.

    • You hope your prodigal will love you for helping.

    • Your prodigal demands your help.

    • You are motivated by tremendous guilt.

2. What patterns do you detect in your prodigal's problems?
    What patterns do you see in the ways you attempt to fix
    those problems?

3. In what ways have your attempts to fix problems been a hindrance to God's redemptive work in your prodigal's life?

4. Has this chapter given you a fresh perspective on rescuing your prodigal? If so, how?

5. Write out your analysis and plan based on these questions:

   • How have you been irresponsible in fixing the problems?

   • How has that hurt your prodigal?

   • In what ways does your prodigal need to be more responsible?

- What are your decisions about what to do (or not do) from now on?

- How will your prodigal probably respond to your decision?

- How will you respond to your prodigal's reaction?

6. Who can best support you during this time?

7. What tests can you implement to see whether your prodigal is becoming trustworthy?

Chapter 8
PRINCIPLE FIVE:
WATCHING YOUR WORDS

1. In your personal experience, how would you confirm James's statement that "the tongue is a fire" (James 3:6)?

2. What are some recent verbal messages you have given your prodigal? Can you think of any nonverbal ones? How did he or she respond to each?

3. What are some specific things you appreciate or admire about your prodigal? (Think of work, talents, hobbies, relationships, and any other area of life.)

4. Talk to ten people and ask *them* what messages you have communicated to or about your prodigal. Summarize their comments below.

5. Ask your prodigal what messages you have communicated to him or her. Write a paragraph here to summarize what you learned from the conversation.

6. What specific steps will you take to stop speaking destructive words and start (or accelerate) the use of affirming words?

7. In terms of a farmer's expectations and patience, what can you expect as you try to relate more positively to your prodigal?

Chapter 9

PRINCIPLE SIX:
PRAYING THE HARD PRAYERS

1. Describe the history of your prayers for your prodigal. When have you felt confident of God's hand at work? When has your faith wavered?

2. Write your own prayer according to these openings:

   • Lord, use my prodigal's friends.

   • Lord, change me first.

- Lord, give me a fresh perspective.

- Lord, I ask for brokenness.

- Lord, help me fight the battle.

- Lord, don't let me give up.

- Lord, whatever it takes . . .

Chapter 10
HOPING FOR THE END OF THE JOURNEY

1. Describe some of the times in your relationship with your prodigal when you have been tempted to give up on God and stop trusting Him.

2. How does the idea of "waiting on the Lord" encourage you to hang on and trust Him? (Review Psalm 130.)

3. How does it change your perspective to know that someday you will stand before Christ and give an account of your own trust, attitudes, and actions rather than your prodigal's?

5. As we conclude this book, write a prayer to God expressing:

- your thankfulness for His goodness,
- your desire to trust Him no matter what,
- you reluctance to apply any of the principles in this book (be specific),
- your desire to please God by your faithfulness, and
- your hopes for your prodigal.

ACKNOWLEDGMENTS

· · · — — · · ·

AUTHORS WRITE BOOKS for different reasons. Some writers have a story to tell or a point of view to express. Other authors find a subject so interesting that they feel they must share the fruit of their research. Still others take pen in hand because a message burns with passion in their hearts.

This is a book born from passion.

For years I heard countless individuals plead with me to pray for their son or daughter who was away from God. Their voices echoed the desperation and helplessness in their hearts. Someone had to say something.

Someone had to offer hope.

Motivated by a desire to help, my journey for answers took me through numerous books, articles, and recordings. It was only after interviewing several prodigals—those who have returned to serve God as well as some who still live in the "far country"—that I began to find insights to help our sons and daughters return to God.

These insights carried me back to the prodigal son in

Luke 15. As I viewed the story through the eyes and actions of the father, I discovered the principles in this book.

Along the way of preparing these materials, I realized that many people in my life deserve more expressions of gratitude than I could ever give. I want to express my sincere and heartfelt thanks . . .

To my parents, who practiced these principles and prevented me from being a prodigal.

To the staff of Phil Waldrep Ministries, who make my work a joy instead of a chore.

To the staff of Worthy Publishing (with a special thanks to my editor, Kyle Olund). You all shared my passion for making a difference in the lives of people. You are the best!

To my pastor, Dr. Rob Jackson, and my family of faith, the Central Baptist Church in Decatur, Alabama, for their continued love, acceptance, and encouragement.

To the many churches and ministries that partner with us in ministry.

To the pastors, staff, and ministry leaders who continue to bring groups to our conferences. Your trust is a blessing.

To the prodigals who shared their stories and opened their hearts. Thank you for your honesty.

To my friend Pat Springle, who used his professional skills to help me express my message clearly.

And last but not the least, to my wife, Debbie, our two daughters, Maegan and Melodi, our son-in-law, T. C., and my granddaughter, who make being a husband, father, father-in-law, and a grandfather the greatest honor and joy in the world.

This book leaves the presses with a prayer in our hearts for you and your prodigal. It is our sincere desire to help you experience the joy of "killing the fatted calf" when your prodigal comes home.

—Phil Waldrep
Decatur, Alabama
February 2016

ABOUT THE AUTHOR

· · · — — — · · ·

PHIL WALDREP is the president of Phil Waldrep Ministries in Decatur, Alabama. He hosts a weekly online video series and podcast called *Real Life with Phil Waldrep.*

Phil and his wife, Debbie, are the founders of the popular Women of Joy Conferences. Phil also founded the Gridiron Men's Conference as well as the Celebrators Conference, which is designed for mature adults. Phil speaks to audiences each year, helping them address personal and family issues from a biblical perspective.

Phil is a dedicated family man, and he and Debbie have two grown children and one grandchild.

For more information, visit:
www.PhilWaldrep.org

WE WANT TO JOIN YOU AS YOU PRAY FOR YOUR PRODIGAL

Get a **FREE** set of prayer cards when you visit philwaldrep.org/prodigal and sign up to receive *Reaching Your Prodigal: A Six-Month Journey of Prayer*.

Have a prayer request or a story of redemption to share? We would love to hear it!

Visit philwaldrep.org/prodigal and click the share button.

REAL LIFE
with Phil Waldrep

Real Life with Phil Waldrep is a
weekly video devotional that meets
you where you are - on your
computer, tablet, or phone.

Visit **philwaldrep.org/reallife** to
subscribe for free!

DOWNLOAD THE APP!

Stream Real Life with Phil Waldrep from your
mobile device wherever you are.

Search for Real Life with Phil Waldrep in the app
store on your Apple, Android, or Windows Phone
device and download it for free!

PHIL WALDREP MINISTRIES
ENCOURAGEMENT FOR LIFE

FIND MORE GREAT RESOURCES ONLINE!
www.philwaldrep.org

KEEP IN TOUCH WITH PHIL.

@philwaldrep

facebook.com/philwaldrep

prodigal@philwaldrep.org

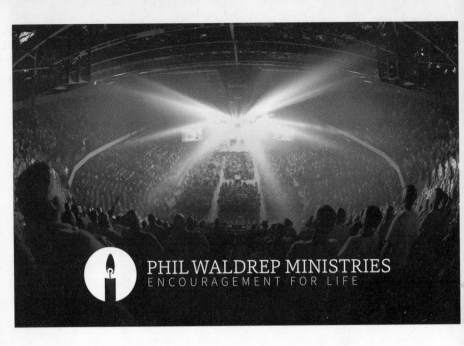

PHIL WALDREP MINISTRIES
ENCOURAGEMENT FOR LIFE

CONFERENCES CRAFTED FOR YOU TO ENCOUNTER THE CREATOR.

www.womenofjoy.org

www.celebrators.org

www.gridironmen.org